麦格希 中英双语阅读文库

动物的故事

【美】比林斯 (Billings, H.)　　【美】比林斯 (Billings, M.) ●主编

杨挺扬 ●译

麦格希中英双语阅读文库编委会 ●编

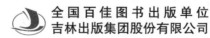

全国百佳图书出版单位

吉林出版集团股份有限公司

图书在版编目（CIP）数据

动物的故事 / (美) 比林斯 (Billings, H.) , (美)比林斯 (Billings, M.) 主编; 杨挺扬译; 麦格希中英双语阅读文库编委会编. -- 2版. -- 长春: 吉林出版集团股份有限公司, 2018.3（2022.1重印）

（麦格希中英双语阅读文库）

ISBN 978-7-5581-4729-6

Ⅰ.①动… Ⅱ.①比… ②比… ③杨… ④麦… Ⅲ.①英语—汉语—对照读物②故事—作品集—世界—现代 Ⅳ.①H319.4: I

中国版本图书馆CIP数据核字(2018)第046075号

动物的故事

编：麦格希中英双语阅读文库编委会
插　画：齐　航　李延霞
责任编辑：朱　玲
封面设计：冯冯翼
开　本：660mm × 960mm　1/16
字　数：220千字
印　张：9.75
版　次：2018年3月第2版
印　次：2022年1月第2次印刷

出　版：吉林出版集团股份有限公司
发　行：吉林出版集团外语教育有限公司
地　址：长春市福祉大路5788号龙腾国际大厦B座7层
　　　　邮编：130011
电　话：总编办：0431-81629929
　　　　发行部：0431-81629927　0431-81629921(Fax)
印　刷：北京一鑫印务有限责任公司

ISBN 978-7-5581-4729-6　　　定价：35.00元

前 言 *PREFACE*

英国思想家培根说过：阅读使人深刻。阅读的真正目的是获取信息，开拓视野和陶冶情操。从语言学习的角度来说，学习语言若没有大量阅读就如隔靴搔痒，因为阅读中的语言是最丰富、最灵活、最具表现力、最符合生活情景的，同时读物中的情节、故事引人入胜，进而能充分调动读者的阅读兴趣，培养读者的文学修养，至此，语言的学习水到渠成。

"麦格希中英双语阅读文库"在世界范围内选材，涉及科普、社会文化、文学名著、传奇故事、成长励志等多个系列，充分满足英语学习者课外阅读之所需，在阅读中学习英语、提高能力。

◎难度适中

本套图书充分照顾读者的英语学习阶段和水平，从读者的阅读兴趣出发，以难易适中的英语语言为立足点，选材精心、编排合理。

◎精品荟萃

本套图书注重经典阅读与实用阅读并举。既包含国内外脍炙人口、耳熟能详的美文，又包含科普、人文、故事、励志类等多学科的精彩文章。

◎功能实用

本套图书充分体现了双语阅读的功能和优势，充分考虑到读者课外阅读的方便，超出核心词表的词汇均出现在使其意义明显的语境之中，并标注释义。

鉴于编者水平有限，凡不周之处，谬误之处，皆欢迎批评教正。

我们真心地希望本套图书承载的文化知识和英语阅读的策略对提高读者的英语著作欣赏水平和英语运用能力有所裨益。

丛书编委会

Contents

1

The Menace of Pit Bulls

Betty Lou Stidham lived in *terror*. She feared the dogs next door to her—two *ferocious* pit bulls. Earlier, these dogs had *mauled* Stidham's own dog. Stidham, who lived alone, asked the city to have the two pit bulls put to sleep. But officials in Memphis, Tennessee, said no. They

The pit bull has been bred for hundreds of years to be a fearless fighter. But now, especially in urban areas, many people feel that this guard dog is too ferocious for its own good.

牛头犬的威胁

几百年来，人们养牛头犬作为勇敢的斗士。但是现在尤其是在城市地区，许多人感到这种看门狗太狂暴了以至于威胁到了自己的安全。

贝蒂·罗·斯蒂德海姆生活在恐惧之中。她害怕邻居养的两条凶猛的牛头犬。以前，这些狗咬伤了斯蒂德海姆的狗。斯蒂德海姆一个人生活，她要求城市主管部门把这两条牛头犬杀死。但是田纳西州孟菲斯的官员说不行，他们说是她的狗导致了那次攻击，因为它的爪子伸过了邻居家的围栏。

terror *n.* 恐惧　　　　　　　　　　　　　ferocious *adj.* 凶猛的
maul *v.* 袭击；撕咬

said her dog had caused the attack. It had stuck its paw through the neighbor's fence.

And so, on a *steamy* day in 1990, Betty Lou Stidham walked out to her mailbox to get the mail. As she walked back toward her house, the two pit bulls struck. Somehow they had gotten outside their chain-link fence. 57-year-old Stidham never had a chance. The *snarling* dogs jumped all over her. Karen Gomez was driving by in her car at the time. "There was this large body [Stidham weighed 200 pounds] with hardly any clothes on," said Gomez. "There was a dog on each side pulling on the body, which seemed lifeless."

But Stidham wasn't dead—not yet. She did what she could to *fend* off the pit bulls. A neighbor who *witnessed* part of the struggle

---

在1990年的一个湿气很重的白天，贝蒂·罗·斯蒂德海姆走到她的邮箱去取信件，当她返回房屋的时候，两条牛头犬发动了攻击。它们不知道怎么挣脱了锁链。57岁的斯蒂德海姆根本不是对手。两条咆哮着的狗跳到了她的身上。凯伦·格麦兹当时正开车经过。"当时的情景是她那高大的身体穿着的[斯蒂德海姆的体重达到200磅]衣服几乎都被撕扯掉了，"格麦兹说，"在她的身体两边各有一条狗死死咬住，她的身体一动不动。"

但是斯蒂德海姆没有死——当时还没有。她尽力抵抗着牛头犬的进攻。一个目击了部分情景的邻居说："[斯蒂德海姆]多次举起右手。她一

---

steamy *adj.* 潮湿的
fend *v.* 挡开；避开

snarl *v.* 咆哮
witness *v.* 目击

said, "At times [Stidham] would raise her right hand up. When she did, [the dogs] would attack the hand. You could tell she was still alive, maybe *barely*."

The neighbor *desperately* wanted to help Stidham. *Grabbing* two brooms, she began to run toward the dogs. But a friend stopped her. "She beat on me with her fists to let her go help," said the friend. "But I couldn't let her do it. They would have killed her too." Meanwhile, someone had called 911. An *ambulance* arrived and rushed Stidham to the hospital. But it was too late. Stidham had lost too much blood. She died four hours later.

Betty Lou Stidham isn't the only person to be attacked by angry pit bulls. In Michigan, a pit bull broke out of its owner's backyard. It went into a neighbor's yard where young Kyle Corullo was playing.

这样做，[狗]就会攻击她的右手。能看出来当时她还活着，也许是仅仅剩下一口气。"

邻居极力想冲上去帮助斯蒂德海姆。她抓起了两把扫帚，开始向狗冲了过去。但是一个朋友阻止了她。"她用她的拳头打着我，要去帮助，"那位朋友说，"但是我不能让她那样做。它们可能也会把她咬死。"同时有人打了911。一辆救护车到达，把斯蒂德海姆送到了医院。但是已经太晚了。斯蒂德海姆失血过多，4个小时后她死了。

贝蒂·罗·斯蒂德海姆不是愤怒的牛头犬攻击下死亡的唯一一个。在密歇根州一条牛头犬闯出了主人的后院。进入了邻居的庭院，当时小男孩

---

barely *adv.* 仅仅
grab *v.* 抓

desperately *adv.* 拼命地
ambulance *n.* 救护车

The pit bull killed the little boy by breaking his neck. In Alabama, two pit bulls attacked Johnny Ford as he *jogged*. Ford, who was the city's mayor, saved himself by climbing up a tree. Still, the dogs did plenty of damage. They nearly *ripped* off one of Ford's legs.

Dozens of people have been mauled or killed by pit bulls in recent years. What makes these dogs so *vicious*? Pit bulls—which are really bull terriers—are strongly built. And they have been bred to be fierce. It has been said that a pit bull would rather fight than eat. In the 1800s, some owners set up fights between these dogs. Two dogs would be put into a pit. They would fight while people, who bet on one dog or the other, cheered.

Although pit bull fighting is now against the law, some people still use the dogs as fighters. Some use the dogs for protection. They

---

凯尔·库鲁罗正在玩耍。那条牛头犬扭断孩子的脖子杀死了小孩。在阿拉巴马州，约翰尼·福特当时正在跑步，两条牛头犬向他发动了攻击。福特是城市的市长。爬上了树逃了一命。但是狗也造成了大量的破坏。它们几乎把福特的一条腿扯了下来。

在近些年，有几十人被牛头犬咬伤或者咬死。是什么使这些狗如此凶暴？牛头犬——是真正的牛头猎犬——身体十分强壮。养育它们的方式目的就在于培养凶残。据说，牛头犬宁可战斗也不去吃食。在19世纪，一些狗的主人设立了一些赛狗的比赛。两条狗放到了同一个坑里。它们会大咬出口，而人们会为一条或者另一条狗下注，欢呼。

虽然现在牛头犬斗狗违法，但是一些人仍然使用这种狗作为斗狗。有些人养狗来看家护院，他们养牛头犬作为看门狗；而另一些人就是喜欢

---

jog *v.* 慢跑

vicious *adj.* 恶毒的

rip *v.* 撕

keep pit bulls as guard dogs. Others just like the breed. They say that a well-trained pit bull can make a *marvelous* pet. They are loyal and they love to be around people. "There's no dog that has a bigger heart," said one pit bull owner. "You can just feel the love coming from this dog."

In fact, many dog experts claim that the problem lies not with the dogs but with the owners. Some people treat their pit bulls badly. Others don't bother to train the dogs properly. So perhaps the owners are to blame for pit bull attacks. Today, owners in some places face *fines* or even *jail* if their pit bulls attack someone.

So, is the pit bull a good dog or a bad dog? It depends. If the dog is curled up on your lap by the fire, it's a good dog. But if it's tearing at your arm, it's a real *menace*.

这个品种。他们说一条训练良好的牛头犬可以是一个绝好的宠物。它们忠诚，并且喜欢在人的周围。"再没有别的狗能有这样的心灵，"一名牛头犬的主人说，"你能够感受到这条狗所发出的爱意。"

实际上，许多狗类专家说，问题不在于狗，而在于人。一些人对他们牛头犬的态度很糟糕。一些人没有适当地训练他们的狗。所以对于牛头犬的攻击，那些主人是应当受到指责的。今天在一些地方如果发生牛头犬伤人的事件，他们的主人会面临着罚款甚至入狱的可能。

那么牛头犬是一种好狗还是坏狗？这可说不准。如果狗在壁炉边，你的脚边蜷起身子，那就是一条好狗。但是如果它撕咬你的胳膊，那就真是糟糕了。

---

marvelous *adj.* 了不起的；非凡的
jail *n.* 监狱

fine *n.* 罚款
menace *n.* 威胁；恐吓

2

A Whale of a Tale

On August 12, 1819, a whaling ship called the Essex sailed from New England. *On board* were 20 men. They were whalers, men who killed whales for their *valuable* oil. The men planned to be at sea for two and a half years. In the first 15 months, things went smoothly. The whalers found and

Nineteenth-century whalers hunted whales for their oil, bones, and meat. Hunting huge whales in small, unprotected boats was a risky way to make a living.

一条鲸鱼,一个故事

19世纪的捕鲸人通过捕杀鲸鱼来获得鲸油、鲸骨和肉。用没有任何保护的小船来捕杀巨大的鲸鱼是一种非常危险的谋生方式。

1819年8月12日,一艘叫作"埃塞克斯"的捕鲸船从新英格兰出发了。船上有20个人。他们都是捕鲸人,捕杀鲸鱼是为了获得具有经济价值的鲸油。他们几乎要在海上生活两年半的时间。在最初的15个月里,一切

---

on board 在船上　　　　　　　　　　　　valuable *adj.* 有价值的

killed 25 whales. But on November 20, 1820, everything changed. On that day, a whale fought back. Suddenly, the hunters became the hunted.

The crew of the Essex was used to working in dangerous conditions. After all, they could not do their job from the *deck* of the main ship. If they could have, the job would have been a lot easier. The Essex was a *sturdy* 238 tons. Instead, the men had to get right next to the whales. They needed to get close enough to *plunge* their *harpoons* into the creatures' sides. So they had to leave the Essex and do their hunting in small whaleboats. These boats were just 28 feet long and 6 feet wide. They didn't weigh much, either. They were made from planks of wood that were less than half an inch thick.

In these small boats, the men went after giant sperm whales.

顺利。捕鲸的人们找到并且杀死了25条鲸鱼。但是在1820年11月20日，一切都变了。在那一天，一条鲸鱼进行了反击。突然，猎人变成了猎物。

"埃塞克斯号"上的船员们已经习惯于在危险的环境里面工作了。毕竟他们不能从大船的甲板上直接来做活，如果他们可以这样做，工作会简单得多。"埃塞克斯号"有238吨重。实际上，船员们需要来到鲸鱼的旁边。需要足够的近，这样他们可以将鱼叉投刺入鲸鱼的侧面。所以，他们需要离开"埃塞克斯号"，在小型的捕鲸小舟上捕猎。这些小舟仅仅28英尺长6英尺宽。它们也不很重。它们是一些不足半英寸厚的木板制作的。

捕鲸人就是驾驶着这样的小舟追踪着巨大的抹香鲸。一头成熟的抹香

---

deck *n.* 甲板
plunge *v.* 猛力插入；扎进

sturdy *adj.* 结实的
harpoon *n.* 鱼叉

An adult sperm whale might measure well over 80 feet—almost the length of the Essex itself. Its tail could be 20 feet wide. If a whale's tail ever hit one of the *fragile* whaleboats, it would *smash* it to bits. So the men had to *maneuver* their boats with great care. On November 20, the Essex was far out in the Pacific Ocean. In the early morning the men spotted whales. Two men stayed on the Essex while the others climbed into three whaleboats. Each boat carried six men. George Pollard, the captain, *commanded* one boat. Owen Chase, the first mate, sailed in the second boat. Matthew Joy, the second mate, led the third boat.

The whalers rowed far from the Essex. They drew closer and closer to the group of sperm whales. Finally, Chase's crew drew alongside one. Chase stood at the bow and plunged his harpoon

---

鲸的长度可能会达到80英尺以上——几乎就是"埃塞克斯号"的长度。它的尾巴可能会达到20英尺宽。如果鲸鱼的尾巴击中那些脆弱的捕鲸小舟，肯定会把它们打成碎片。所以这些人需要极其小心地驾驶这些小舟。11月20日，"埃塞克斯号"来到了太平洋的深处。在清晨，船员们看到了鲸鱼。两个人留在了"埃塞克斯号"上，其他人爬到了3条捕鲸小舟上。每个小舟上面乘坐6个人。船长乔治·伯拉德指挥一条小舟。大副欧文·奇斯指挥第二艘，二副马修·乔伊领导着第三条船。

捕鲸人划船远离了"埃塞克斯号"，它们与一群抹香鲸越来越近了。最后奇斯的船员们来到了一条鲸鱼的旁边。奇斯站在船头，把他的鱼叉投

---

fragile *adj.* 脆的；易碎的
maneuver *v.* 操作

smash *v.* 打碎；粉碎
command *v.* 指挥

into the whale. The whale *flipped* its tail, *grazing* the boat. The blow was enough to punch a hole in the side of the light boat.

Chase knew his men could not continue with the hunt. The other two whaleboats would have to go on alone. Chase cut the line to his harpoon. Then he stuffed the crew's jackets into the gaping hole in the boat. Chase told one man to *bail* out the water. He ordered the others to row back to the Essex as fast as they could.

When they returned to the Essex, Chase began to repair the whaleboat with a piece of canvas. Suddenly, he saw a sperm whale. It was huge. Chase guessed that it was 85 feet long. The creature was just 100 yards away. Yet Chase was not worried. Whales are not vicious. In fact, most of the time they are rather playful.

There was nothing playful about this whale, however. It *spouted*

向那条鲸鱼。那条鲸鱼抽打着尾巴,擦伤了小舟。这一击已经足够在小舟的旁边打出一个洞。

奇斯知道他的手下人已经不能继续捕猎了。另外两艘小舟可以继续追击。奇斯割断了系在鱼叉上的绳索,然后他用船员的衣服塞住了船上的洞。奇斯让一个人把船里面的水向外面舀,命令其他人尽快划回"埃塞克斯号"。

当它们回到"埃塞克斯号"时,奇斯开始用一块帆布修理捕鲸舟。突然他见到了一条巨大的抹香鲸,体态十分庞大。奇斯猜想它可能有85英尺长。它距离他们只有100码。但是奇斯并没有担心,因为鲸鱼并不凶猛。实际上大部分时间它们十分喜欢玩耍。

但是这条鲸鱼可不是玩什么游戏。它喷了两三次水后在水面上消失

---

flip *v.* 快速猛然移动(某物)

bail *v.* 往外舀水

graze *v.* 擦伤

spout *v.* 喷出

two or three times then disappeared below the surface. When it came up again, it was only 30 yards away. The whale was moving straight at the Essex. Chase couldn't believe his eyes. He ordered one of his men to steer the Essex out of the way. But it was too late. The giant whale *rammed* into the ship with its massive 20-foot head. The blow knocked the men to their knees. They all looked at each other in amazement. No one spoke. No one knew what to say. They had never heard of a whale attacking a ship before. And this whale wasn't finished. After hitting the ship, the whale swam under it. Moments later, it came up on the other side. It appeared *dazed*. It *thrashed* about, opening and *snapping* its huge jaws. Then one of the men shouted, "Here he is—he is making for us again."

It didn't seem possible. But the whale was attacking the Essex

了。当它再次出现时，距离他们只有30码远了。这条鲸鱼径直向"埃塞克斯号"撞了过来。奇斯无法相信他的眼睛。他命令一名船员调转"埃塞克斯号"的航向，但是太晚了。巨大的鲸鱼的20英尺长的头部重重地撞击在船上。这次撞击使所有的人都跌倒了。他们惊奇地相互对视着，没有人说话，也没有人知道该说什么。他们以前从来没有听说过鲸鱼袭击船只，而且这条鲸鱼没有停止。撞到了船后，它又钻到了船的下面。过了一会，它又在另一边出现了。看起来它有些茫然。它摇晃着，张开了嘴巨大的下巴猛咬了几下。这时一个人喊道："那里——他又来了。"

看起来好像是不可能的。但是，这条鲸鱼开始了第二次对"埃塞克斯

ram v. 撞击某物
thrash v. 猛烈摆动

dazed adj. 茫然的
snap v. 猛咬

a second time. It charged at the ship with twice the speed of the first attack. It lifted its blunt head half out of the water. *Foamy* waves kicked up on both sides as the whale gained speed and *fury*.

This time the whale hit the ship with such force that it crushed the bow. Chase knew the Essex was *doomed*. He told his men to jump into a whaleboat. In a few moments, they rowed safely away. The men watched silently as the ship tipped over on its side.

For the whale, the story ends there. The creature was never seen again. But for the men of the Essex, the story was just beginning. When the two other whaleboats returned from the hunt, the men were *stunned* to find the Essex lying on its side. The whalers got back on the ship for a brief time. They grabbed some sails. They also rescued some biscuits, water, a few guns, tools, and nails.

号"的攻击。它以第一次两倍的速度冲向了"埃塞克斯号"。它钝形的头抬出了水面,随着鲸鱼愤怒地加速,两边的水被劈开,泡沫飞溅。

这一次,鲸鱼很重地撞到了船,把船首撞裂了。奇斯知道"埃塞克斯号"气数已尽。他告诉他的人跳上捕鲸舟。不久,他们安全地划开了。船员们静静地看着船侧翻了。

至于那条鲸鱼,故事也就结束了。它再也没有出现。但是对于"埃塞克斯号"船员来说,故事才刚刚开始。当另外两条捕鲸舟返航时,他们看到"埃塞克斯号"斜躺在水中,都惊呆了。捕鲸人回到了船上简单地检查了一下。他们拿了一些风帆,救出了一些饼干、淡水、枪支、工具和钉子。

---

foamy *adj.* 泡沫的

doom *v.* 注定(死亡、毁灭、失败等)

fury *n.* 狂怒

stun *v.* 使……受惊

But the men faced a *grim* future. They were stuck in three tiny boats in the middle of the ocean. The nearest land was thousands of miles away. It didn't seem likely that they would reach land before they ran out of food and water.

That first day, no one ate. The men had no appetite. Some of them cried. Only a few were able to sleep that night. Most just stared at the black water, wondering what would become of them.

Days passed. Sometimes the wind blew the boats along at a good *pace*. Other times, there was no *breeze* at all. Then the boats just *bobbed* up and down in the water. The hot sun beat down without mercy. It was tough on the men. Some began to lose their will to live. Then, on December 20, one of the men stood up and shouted, "There is land!"

但是他们面临着严峻的未来。他们在海洋的中部被困在3条小舟上面。即使最近的岛屿也是在几千英里以外。看起来在他们的食物和水用光前他们是无法到达陆地的。

第一天，没有人吃东西，他们已经没有胃口了。一些人哭了起来，在晚上只有一些人能够睡得着觉。大部分人只是盯着黑色的海水，想着他们的未来。

几天过去了，有时风可以使船达到一个不错的速度。还有些时候，压根就没有风。那时，船就是在海水中上下飘荡。炎热的太阳毫不留情地晒在人们身上。人们太艰苦了，少数人开始失去了生存的意志。在12月20日，一个人站了起来，大喊道"那是陆地！"

---

grim *adj.* 残忍的
breeze *n.* 微风

pace *n.* 速度
bob *v.* 上下摆动

By *a stroke of pure luck*, the three boats had drifted toward a tiny island. The island wasn't on any map. Today it is known as Henderson's Island.

When the men saw the land, their hopes *surged*. They were saved! But they weren't. The island had fresh water, but almost no food. There wasn't nearly enough to keep 20 men alive. So, after a week, Pollard told the men they would be better off getting back into the whaleboats. Three men refused. They *vowed* to take their chances staying on the island.

These three men were lucky. They were later rescued. But the 17 who sailed off were not so *fortunate*. They drifted for nearly two more months. Some of the men died of hunger. To survive, the others ate the flesh of those who died.

突然被幸运之神光顾，3条船向着这个小岛漂了过去。在任何地图上都没有这个小岛。今天我们称它亨德逊岛。

当人们看到小岛时，希望喷涌了出来。他们得救了！但他们没有。岛上有淡水，但是几乎没有食物来保证20人的生存。这样过了一个星期后，伯拉德告诉船员们他们最后还是决定出海。3个人拒绝了，他们许愿要呆在这个岛上听天由命。

这3个人很幸运，后来获得了营救。但是那17个出海的人就没有那么幸运了。他们几乎漂流了两个月。其中的一些人死于饥饿。为了生存，活着的人吃死去人的肉。

a stroke of pure luck 鸿运当头
vow v. 许愿

surge v. 激增；急剧上升
fortunate adj. 幸运的

In time, the wind blew the three boats far away from each other. One was never seen again. On February 17, 1821, a passing ship *spotted* one of the whaleboats. It contained Chase and two other men. Six days later, a different ship rescued Pollard and one other from the third whaleboat. These *survivors* had been in their tiny boats for three months and had sailed 3,000 miles.

In all, only eight members of the crew survived. Twelve died at sea. The sad story of the Essex did have one bright spot, however. It inspired one of the great novels of all time. After learning about the whale's bizarre attack, author Herman Melville wrote a similar story in his classic book, *Moby Dick*.

当时，风把3条船吹散了，其中一艘船再也没有见到。在1821年2月17日，一艘经过的船只看到了一条捕鲸舟，上面有奇斯和另外的两个人。6天后，另一艘船营救了伯拉德和另一个人，他们在第三条船上。这些获救者已经在他们的小船上呆了3个月，漂流了3000英里。

最终，船员中只有8人获救。12人死在了海上。"埃塞克斯号"的悲惨故事也有一个好的方面。它激发了当时的一位伟大的小说作家赫尔曼·麦尔维尔，他研究了鲸鱼奇怪的攻击行为后，在他的著名小说《白鲸》中写了一个相似的故事。

---

spot *v.* 认出   survivor *n.* 幸存者

3

Grizzly Tales

Bill Riodan didn't see the bear until it was too late. Riodan had been out hunting deer in the Alaskan woods. On his way home, he came to a big *spruce* tree lying on the ground. He set his gun down and began to climb over the fallen tree. As he did so, a huge *paw* reached up from the other side of the log. Riodan felt

The adult grizzly bear can grow more than eight feet tall and weigh more than 1,500 pounds. While on a hike in the western states or Alaska, you'd better hope you don't run into one of these unpredictable animals.

灰熊的故事

成年的灰熊能够长到8英尺高，体重达到1500磅。如果你在西部州或者阿拉斯加旅行，你最好希望不要遇到这些无法预料的动物。

直到一切都太晚的时候，比尔·罗丹才见到熊。罗丹来到了阿拉斯加的森林中捕鹿。在他回家的路上，他来到了一棵巨大的倒下的云杉树前面，他放下了枪开始爬过倒下的树。正当他爬的时候，从树的另一边伸出了一只巨大的爪子。罗丹感到一阵恐慌涌上了他的胸口。他就在一个灰熊

---

spruce *n.* 云杉   paw *n.* 爪子

panic rising in his chest. He was *perched* right over the den of a *grizzly* bear! With a quick *swipe*, the bear dug her claws into Riodan's back and pulled him down to the ground.

There was nothing Riodan could do. The bear began to *rip* open his body. She took bite after bite from his arms, neck, and back. She ate chunks of flesh the size of fists. In effect, the bear was eating him alive!

Within a few minutes, Riodan passed out. When he awoke, the bear was still there. Now her two cubs were poking at him. Riodan tried to get up, but as soon as he moved, the mother bear pounced on him again. She grabbed him by the leg and shook him, crushing his leg bone between her jaws.

Again Riodan passed out. The next time he woke up, it was night. He didn't know if the bears had gone away or were just sleeping.

洞穴的上面！灰熊的爪子一扫，扫在了他的背部，把他击倒在地。

当时，罗丹无能为力。熊开始撕开他的身体，它一口又一口地咬着他的胳膊、颈部和后背。它吃着拳头大小的肉。实际上，熊正在生吞活剥着他！

几分钟之内，罗丹晕了过去。当他醒过来时熊还在那里。现在它的两头幼崽正在摆弄着他。罗丹试图起来，但是他一动，母熊就再次向他发动了攻击。它咬住了他的腿，开始甩动，它的嘴把他的腿骨弄碎。

罗丹再次昏了过去。他再次苏醒过来时是在晚上。他不知道熊是在

---

perch *v.* 栖息；位于

swipe *n.* 猛击

grizzly *adj.* 灰色的

rip *v.* 撕

Slowly, quietly, he crawled away. He dragged himself to a *creek*. Hours later, friends found him there, inching his way downstream.

Riodan's body was covered with 42 wounds. Muscles had been torn from his shoulders, arms, and neck. His leg was badly *mangled*. He was lucky to be alive. Doctors said it was the creek that saved him. The *mud* and leaves there helped *seal* the wounds and stop the bleeding.

Bill Riodan's brush with death came in the fall of 1908. Riodan was not the first person to be attacked by a bear. And he certainly wasn't the last. Every year or two, someone is killed in a bear attack. Often the killer is a grizzly. These animals, also called Alaskan brown bears, are found throughout the western United States. They are huge creatures. In fact, they are the largest meat-eating animal that lives on land. Standing over eight feet tall, they can weigh up to 1,500 pounds. Sometimes they run away when they see a human

---

睡觉还是走开了。他缓慢，静静地爬走了。他爬到了小溪旁边。几个小时后，他的朋友们找到了他，当时他正在沿着小溪缓慢地爬行。

罗丹的身体上面有42处伤口。肩膀、胳膊和颈部的肌肉被撕掉了。腿受到严重的损伤。他能够活下来很幸运。医生说小溪救了他的命。那里的泥和树叶帮助了伤口的愈合，止住了流血。

比尔·罗丹与死神的擦肩而过是在1908年的秋季。罗丹不是第一个受到熊攻击的人，当然他也不是最后一个。每一两年，都会有一个人在熊的攻击下丧生。常见的杀手是灰熊。这种动物也被称作阿拉斯加棕熊，在整个美国西部都有分布。它们的体形十分巨大。实际上它们是世界上最大型的食肉动物。站起来它们有8英尺高，体重可以达到1500磅。看到人

---

creek *n.* 小溪
mud *n.* 泥

mangle *v.* 损坏
seal *v.* 愈合

being. But sometimes they attack.

Deane and Lorraine Lengkeek found that out the hard way. They were walking through Montana's Glacier National Park on August 30, 1991. As they *rounded* a *bend*, they saw a mother grizzly and her two cubs. The Lengkeeks dropped to the ground. They had heard that the best way to avoid a bear attack was to play dead.

But this mama bear was not fooled. She gave a low *growl*. Then she raced over to Deane Lengkeek. She bit into his side with her enormous yellow teeth. Holding him in her mouth, she shook her head a couple of times. Then she threw him into the air. When he hit the ground, she picked him up again. She began to *haul* him back into the bushes.

"Oh, dear God, not like this!" he cried out. "Please, not like this!"

Lorraine Lengkeek was terrified. She did the only thing she could

---

时，有时它们会逃跑，但是有时会攻击。

狄恩和劳林·隆奇克经历了这种危险境地。1991年8月30日，他们当时正在步行通过蒙大拿的国家冰川公园。当他们走过一处弯道时，看见一头母熊和它的两个幼崽，隆奇克夫妇马上倒在地上，他们听说过最好的躲避熊攻击的方法是装死。

但是这头母熊没有上当。她低沉地吼叫了一声，然后冲到了狄恩·隆奇克的身边，它黄色的牙齿一口咬到了他的体侧。它把他叼了起来，在空中甩动了几次，然后把他扔到了空中。他一落地，它又把他叼了起来。它开始把他拖回树林。

"啊，天哪！不要这样！"他大喊道，"不要这样！"

劳林·隆奇克被吓坏了。她唯一能做的就是想该怎么办。她追在熊的

---

round *v.* 绕行　　　　　　　　　　bend *n.* 弯曲处

growl *n.* 咆哮；吼　　　　　　　　haul *v.* 拖

think of to do. She ran after the bear, swinging her *binoculars* over her head. When she got close, she hit the animal's nose with the binoculars. After four blows, the grizzly dropped Deane. Now the bear turned toward Lorraine. Lorraine *swung* the binoculars again. After this blow, the grizzly finally turned and ran off.

Deane Lengkeek was badly hurt, but he survived. He owed his life to his wife's brave actions. Perhaps Lorraine was successful because she targeted the nose. It is a very *sensitive* part of a bear's body. Bears don't have good eyesight. They can't hear well, either. So they rely heavily on their keen sense of smell. They need their long noses to help them *sniff* out danger and food. Sometimes when a bear's nose is hurt, the bear retreats. A few people have fought off bears by jamming their fingers into bears' nostrils.

Sometimes, though, bears have been almost impossible to stop.

后面, 在头上挥舞着她的双筒望远镜。当她离近时, 她用双筒望远镜击中了熊的鼻子。打了4下后, 熊放下了狄恩。现在熊转过身来对付劳林, 劳林再次挥舞起了双筒望远镜。再次打了一下后, 灰熊最终转过身子逃跑了。

狄恩·隆奇克受了重伤, 但是他活了下来, 是他妻子勇敢的行为救了他一命。劳林能够成功因为她的目标是熊的鼻子, 那是熊身上极为敏感的部分。熊的视力不好, 它们的听觉也不好。所以它们十分依赖它们敏锐的嗅觉。它们需要长长的鼻子来嗅出危险和食物。有时当熊的鼻子受到伤害时, 它们会退缩。已经有几个人通过用手指塞住熊的鼻道把熊赶跑。

有时, 熊几乎是无法阻止的。1905年, 3名阿拉斯加人向一头攻击他

---

binocular *n.* 双筒望远镜　　　　swing *v.* 挥舞
sensitive *adj.* 敏感的　　　　sniff *v.* 嗅

In 1905, three Alaskans began shooting at a grizzly that attacked them. Thirteen times they struck the bear with bullets. Again and again the bear fell down. But each time it got back up. Finally, after the 14th shot, the bear dropped to the ground *for good*.

Claude Barnes had his rifle in his hands when a grizzly came at him. Barnes was out hunting in the Wyoming woods. He had just taken a shot at a small bear. The mother bear heard its *yelp*. She came charging toward Barnes. Said Barnes, "I shot at her heart while she ... stood towering over me." That didn't stop her, though. She dropped onto all fours and kept coming. "I *reloaded* as quickly as I could and fired into her face. She was right on me ... she grabbed the gun *barrel* with her teeth [and] knocked me down with her body. ... Her great jaws [sank] into my side just below my right shoulder. ... A huge foot was placed on my shoulders and I could smell the hot breath of

们的灰熊开枪，子弹13次击中了这只灰熊。熊一次又一次地跌倒。但是每一次熊都起来了，最后开了第十四枪后，熊才倒在地上死了。

当灰熊袭击克劳德·巴恩斯时，他的手里拿着一支猎枪。巴恩斯在怀俄明州的森林里面打猎。他刚刚向一只小熊开了一枪。母熊听到了它的叫声，跑过来向巴恩斯冲了上来。巴恩斯说："我向她的心脏开了一枪但是她……高高地站在我的上方。"那并没有止住它。她四脚着地继续向前冲。"我迅速地重新装弹，向它的脸部开了一枪。它就在我的前面……她一口咬住了枪管而且用身体把我撞倒……它巨大的下巴陷入了我的右肩下部……巨大的脚掌踩住了我的肩膀，我能够闻到一股强烈的兽性气味。"

for good 永久地

reload *v.* 再装填弹药

yelp *n.* （通常因害怕或痛苦）尖叫

barrel *n.* 枪管

the tremendous brute."

Barnes had fired two bullets at the bear at very close range. Yet neither one seemed to slow the animal down. Barnes survived only because the bear suddenly turned to check on her wounded cub. Knowing that grizzlies don't climb trees, Barnes scrambled up a nearby pine. The bear tried to reach him, but she couldn't. So she stood on the ground, *clawing* angrily at the trunk. Barnes clung to that tree for hours. At last, his bullets took effect. The bear collapsed, dead, a few feet from the tree.

Game warden Al Johnson also knew that grizzlies don't climb trees. In 1973 Johnson wanted to take some pictures of bear cubs. He climbed 15 feet into a tree, sure that he would be safe there. But he was wrong. A mother grizzly with three cubs came along. When the mother *detected* Johnson's presence, she became *enraged*. She

---

巴恩斯在距离熊很近的地方开了两枪。但是两枪好像都没有减弱它的进攻速度。巴恩斯能够幸存下来完全是因为熊突然回头去查看它受伤的幼崽。巴恩斯知道灰熊不会爬树，他飞快地爬上了附近的一棵松树。熊想抓住他，但是抓不到。它站在地上愤怒地抓挠着树干。巴恩斯被困在树上达到几个小时。最后他的子弹起了作用。熊倒在地上，死了，离树仅仅几英尺。

护林员艾尔·约翰逊也知道灰熊不会爬树。1973年，约翰逊打算拍一些熊幼崽的照片。他爬到一棵树的15英尺高处，确保他在那里能够安全。但是他错了。一头母熊带着三头幼崽走了过来。当母熊发现约翰逊在那里时，它变得极其暴躁。它愤怒地冲向了那棵树。它尽力地爬得足够高

---

claw *v.* 用爪子抓

enraged *adj.* 暴怒的

detect *v.* 发现

flew at the tree with fury. She managed to get high enough to pull Johnson to the ground. She bit his shoulder, arms, and elbow. Then she tore a patch of skin off his *scalp*. He heard her teeth *scraping* against his skull. At last, the bear turned away. Rather than finish Johnson off, she chose to lead her cubs away to safety.

Could any of these attacks have been prevented? Perhaps. Bears usually don't *pounce* unless they feel threatened. Claude Barnes *provoked* his attacker by shooting at her cub. Bill Riodan upset his bear by coming too close to her nest. The problem is that it doesn't take much to threaten a bear.

Just going into the woods can do it. That's all Deane and Lorraine Lengkeek did. And it's all Al Johnson did. So the next time you're out enjoying a nature walk, keep your fingers crossed that you don't cross paths with a grizzly.

把约翰逊拉到了地面。它咬了他的肩膀、胳膊和肘部。然后它又撕开了他的头皮。他能够听到它的牙齿与他头盖骨的摩擦声。最后熊离开了。它没有杀死约翰逊，它选择了把它的幼崽带走，带到安全的地方。

这些攻击能够避免吗？也许可以。只有在感到受威胁时，熊才会发动攻击。克劳德·巴恩斯枪击小熊激起了母熊的攻击。比尔·罗丹距离熊的巢穴太近了，使熊攻击。问题是，不需要什么行动就可能威胁到熊。

就连到树林里面去就可能出现这样的效果。而这正是狄恩和劳林·隆奇克的所作所为，也是艾尔·约翰逊所做的事情。所以下一次当你到外面享受在大自然中的散步时，请你祷告不要通过灰熊的路线。

---

scalp *n.* 头皮

pounce *v.* 突袭；猛扑

scrape *v.* 刮出刺耳声

provoke *v.* 激怒；惹起

Attack of the Red Fire Ants

In Alabama a newborn baby was killed while lying in a *crib*. In Florida a little girl lost her life as she played with her dog. In Louisiana an old man died after being attacked in a *motel* room. What did these victims have in common? They were all killed by red fire ants.

At first glance these ants don't look

The red fire ant is so small that you can't see it well without a powerful electron microscope. However, these ants have been causing big problems in the Southeast and are now traveling to other states too.

红火蚂蚁的袭击

红火蚂蚁很小，如果没有强大的电子显微镜你无法把它看得很清楚。但是这些蚂蚁却在东南部导致了巨大的问题，而且现在正在影响到其他的州。

阿拉巴马州，一个新生的婴儿在摇篮里面被杀。佛罗里达州，一个小女孩在与她的狗玩耍时丧生。路易斯安娜州，一个老年人在汽车旅馆的房间里面受到袭击丧生。这些受害者有什么共同之处呢？他们都是被红火蚂蚁杀死的。

刚开始一看，这些蚂蚁并不十分危险。他们很小——仅仅有一寸的八

crib *n.* 婴儿床

motel *n.* 汽车旅馆

very dangerous. They are small—only about an eighth of an inch long. They have big heads and skinny legs. But the size and shape of the ants is not the problem. The little *critters* have a couple of secret weapons. First of all, each ant has two claws near its mouth. It can use these claws to grab onto your skin. Also, it has a *stinger* at the back end of its body. This stinger carries poison. As the ant clings to your skin, it can shoot the poison right into you.

The sting of a single red fire ant does not hurt that much. According to one researcher, "It [is] worse than a mosquito bite but nowhere near as bad as a *wasp* sting." But the sting is only the beginning. As the poison enters your body, your skin will start to itch. The itching will build to a burning feeling. Finally, a yellow blister will break out at the spot where you were stung. This *nasty* blister

---

分之一大小。他们的脑袋很大，腿很细小，但是这种蚂蚁的大小和形状却不是问题。这种小东西有几个秘密武器。首先，每个蚂蚁的嘴边都有两个爪子，它能够使用这两个爪子抓住你的皮肤。而且它的尾部有一个针，针中有毒。如果蚂蚁爬到了你的身上，它可以直接给你注射毒液。

仅仅一只红火蚂蚁的叮刺并不重要。按照一个研究人员的说法："这要比蚊子叮咬的厉害，但是没有黄蜂叮咬那么严重。"但是叮刺只是开始。随着毒液进入你的身体，你的皮肤将开始发痒，这种发痒是火辣辣的。最后，受叮刺的地方会出现一个黄色的水泡。这个令人难受的水泡可

---

critter *n.* 生物

wasp *n.* 黄蜂

stinger *n.* 螫针

nasty *adj.* 令人厌恶的

can *linger* for days, even weeks. It will itch like crazy. But beware: scratching will only make it worse. The blister could become infected. You could end up *scarred* for the rest of your life.

One fire ant sting is bad enough. But you almost never get stung once. When a red fire ant attacks, it stings again and again. And these ants don't travel alone. So when one *latches* onto you, you can be pretty sure that dozens of others will join in. In just a few seconds, you can be covered with a whole swarm of stinging ants.

Marion Bernhardt found that out the hard way. She was lying in a Florida hospital in 1994. Suddenly, from out of nowhere, red fire ants began to crawl all over her. Said Bernhardt, "I was stung all up and down my legs, and I had *welts* all over them and on my side. They burned for days. I never had such an experience in all my life." Many

---

能会持续几天，甚至几个星期。它会极其发痒。但是注意：抓挠只会使事情更糟。水泡会感染。你的后半生会一直留有伤疤。

　　一只红火蚂蚁的叮刺已经足够糟糕的了。但是你几乎不可能只受一次叮刺。当红火蚂蚁攻击时，它叮了一次又一次。而且这些蚂蚁不是单独出现。所以当你的身上出现一只蚂蚁时，你几乎可以肯定还有几十只将会加入。就在几秒钟内你可能就被一整群叮咬的蚂蚁盖住。

　　马里昂·波恩哈德很痛苦地发现了这个问题。在1994年，她在佛罗里达医院卧在床上。突然之间，红火蚂蚁开始爬遍了她的全身。波恩哈德说："我的腿上被叮咬个遍，腿上满是伤痕，我的侧面也是。它们几天都火辣辣地疼。我的一生中从来没有过这样的经历。"许多人同情波恩哈

---

linger *v.* 继续存留　　　　　　　scar *v.* 留下伤疤
latch *v.* 纠缠住某人　　　　　　welt *n.* 伤痕

people can *sympathize* with Bernhardt. Each year, more than 60,000 victims seek medical help after being stung by red fire ants. Millions of others suffer quietly at home.

Marion Bernhardt didn't die from her stings. Most people don't. They can get stung hundreds of times and still walk away. But others react more strongly to the poison. For them, red fire ants can spell death. These people may have trouble breathing after they've been stung. They may pass out or go into shock. Before you know it, they're dead. Red fire ant stings have caused the deaths of more than 85 people in the United States since the 1930s.

Human beings are not the only targets of red fire ants. The ants will go after *beetles*, rats, birds, even small cows. Their goal is to kill and then eat their victims. One of their favorite meals is the flesh of

德。每一年，六万多受害者在受到红火蚂蚁的叮咬后要寻求医生的帮助。几百万的其他受害者在家里默默忍受着。

马里昂·波恩哈德没有死于她受的叮咬。大部分的人都不会死的，他们可以成千上万次被叮咬，还能够走路。但是另一些人对毒素的反应要强烈得多。对于他们来说，红火蚂蚁就代表着死亡。他们被叮咬后，可能会出现呼吸困难。他们可能会昏过去或者休克。在你意识到之前，他们已经死了。从20世纪30年代开始，红火蚂蚁的叮咬导致了美国超过85人的死亡。

人类不是红火蚂蚁唯一的攻击目标。他们会袭击甲虫、老鼠、鸟类甚至小牛。它们的目标是杀死然后吃掉它们的受害者。它们最喜欢的大餐是

sympathize *v.* 同情   beetle *n.* 甲虫

young deer. Fire ants find these deer quite easy to kill. When a *fawn* is threatened, it stands perfectly still. That allows the fire ants to climb onto it. They sting it everywhere—on its legs, its stomach, its neck. As the ants sting the fawn near its eyes, it becomes *blinded*. Finally, it reacts by trying to lick the ants off its body. But that just makes matters worse. The ants keep *ejecting* their poison even as they are swallowed. They sting the inside of the deer's mouth. They sting its throat, windpipe, and stomach. Soon these body parts swell up so that the fawn can no longer breathe. Within minutes, it is dead.

Americans didn't always have to worry about red fire ants. Before 1930 there were none in the United States. They made their homes in the forests of Brazil. But one day the ants got onto a ship *bound for* Alabama. When the ship docked, the ants came pouring out onto

---

小鹿的肉。红火蚂蚁发现这些小鹿很容易弄死。当小鹿受到惊吓时，它会完全一动不动。这样使红火蚂蚁能够爬到它的身上。它们会在它的全身进行叮咬——腿上、肚子上、脖子上。如果蚂蚁在眼睛附近叮刺，就会导致失明。最后，鹿的反应是试图把蚂蚁舔掉。但是这只是使事情变糟。即使蚂蚁被吞了进去，它们还是在不断地注射毒液。它们会叮咬鹿嘴的里面。它们叮咬喉咙、气管和胃。很快这些身体的部分开始肿胀，导致小鹿无法呼吸。几分钟之内，就死了。

美国人不是总在忧虑红火蚂蚁。在1930年以前，在美国没有这种蚂蚁。它们在巴西的森林里面安家落户。但是一天，这种蚂蚁登上了一条开

---

fawn *n.* 小鹿　　　　　　　　　　　　blinded *adj.* 失明的
eject *v.* 喷射出　　　　　　　　　　　bound for 开往……的

the land.

At first, they stayed in the Southeast. They could be found only in Alabama, Mississippi, and Florida. Lately, though, they've turned up in other places. They've slipped into moving *vans* and trucks. Some have made it all the way to California. They've also *crept* north to Tennessee and Virginia.

Red fire ants used to stay outdoors. But as Marion Bernhardt can tell you, they are now coming inside. They get into hospitals and motels. They crawl under the floor *mats* of cars. They cause accidents by stinging drivers. They chew through electrical wires in houses. Some people have even fled their homes to get away from the *dreaded* ants.

As if all this were not enough, there's another problem on the

---

往阿拉巴马州的船。当船停下后，这些蚂蚁蜂拥上了岸。

刚开始，它们呆在东南部，只有阿拉巴马、密西西比和佛罗里达州能够发现。后来它们又来到了其他地区。它们钻进了开动着的小汽车和卡车里面。有一些甚至来到了加利福尼亚。它们也潜入了北方的田纳西和弗吉尼亚州。

红火蚂蚁过去习惯于呆在室外。但是马里昂·波恩哈德告诉你，它们开始适应在室内生存。它们钻进了医院和汽车旅馆里面。它们钻进了汽车的地毯下面。它们叮咬驾驶员导致事故。它们咬开电线。一些人甚至逃离家园来躲避可怕的蚂蚁。

就好像这一切都不够，又出现了另外一个问题。美洲红火蚂蚁出现了

---

van *n.* 小型货车

mat *n.* 垫

creep *v.* 慢慢地移动

dreaded *adj.* 可怕的

horizon. Something creepy is going on with America's red fire ants. In the past, these ants formed regular ant *colonies*. Each colony had a single queen. She was the only one who could lay eggs. The rest of the ants in the group would fight to protect her. They would kill any other queen who came near. Because of this, each colony built its *mound* far away from any other colony.

Now that is changing. No one knows why, but some colonies are beginning to accept more than one queen. As many as 500 queens have been found in a single mound. These colonies are huge. One queen can lay 100 eggs an hour. So how many eggs can 500 queens lay? The total is more than a million a day! As these eggs *hatch*, ants *spill* out of the mound and start colonies of their own.

Multiqueen colonies don't mind having neighbors. Again, no

一些神秘的变化。在过去这些蚂蚁会建造普通的蚁穴。每个蚁穴有一个蚁王。它是唯一一个能够产卵的。蚁群中其他的蚂蚁都为它战斗，保护它。如果还有另外的蚁王出现在附近它们就会杀死它。因此一个蚁穴的建造地点与其他蚁穴相距很远。

现在这一切在改变着。没有人知道为什么，但是的确一些蚁穴开始接受多个蚁王。甚至在一个蚁穴中发现了500个蚁王。这样的蚁穴十分巨大。一个蚁王每小时能够下100个卵。那么500个蚁王能够下多少卵？总数是一天一百多万！随着这些卵的孵化，蚂蚁又从这个巢穴中分出来，开始另外建立殖民地。

拥有多个蚁王的巢穴不在乎有无邻居。这个问题还是没有人能够理

---

colony *n.* 殖民地
hatch *v.* 孵化

mound *n.* 土堆；高地
spill *v.* 溢出

one knows why. But ants in these groups don't fight with nearby colonies. So new fire ant mounds are *springing up* right next to old ones. In some places, you can find up to 500 colonies in a single *acre*. Each colony *inhabits* a mound that is about a foot high. Each contains millions of ants. You can just imagine what your backyard would look like if several colonies of fire ants set up house there.

Where will it end? Will red fire ants keep *spreading* across America? Will their colonies keep getting bigger and closer together? It's hard to say. But one thing's for sure. If red fire ants come to your neighborhood, you'll know it!

解。但是这些蚁巢里面的蚂蚁互不相争。旧的蚁巢旁边会建立起一个新的蚁巢。有一些地方在一亩地里面可以找到500个蚁巢。每个蚁巢都有一个土墩，大约有一英尺高。你可以想象，如果红火蚂蚁在你的后院里面筑巢，那里将变成什么样子。

结果会是什么呢？红火蚂蚁会席卷整个美国吗？它们的巢穴会变得越来越大，相互连接吗？很难说。但是有一点是确定的，如果红火蚂蚁来到了你的社区，你会知道的！

---

spring up 出现；涌出   acre *n.* 亩

inhabit *v.* 居住于   spread *v.* 扩散；蔓延

5

Snakes, Snakes Everywhere

You never know where you'll find one. You might see one in your garden in New Jersey. You could spot one in a river in South America. You might even find one in your toilet in India. Some of the snakes you run across may be harmless. But many are dangerous. A few are *downright* deadly. It is *estimated* that snakes kill

This trusting mouse may soon learn a fatal lesson about the eating habits of its companion, the boa constrictor.

毒蛇凶猛

这只轻信的老鼠很快就会学会一个致命的道理，那就是它的同伴，一条大蟒的饮食习惯。

你永远也不知道在哪里会遇到一条蛇。你可能在新泽西家里的花园里面见到一条，也可能在南美的一条河流里面见到一条，甚至在印度的盥洗室里面也能见到一条。你遇到的一些蛇可能是无害的。但是许多都十分危险。一些绝对是致命的。据估计每年蛇会杀死15,000人。

downright *adv.* 完全地　　　　　　　　　　　　estimate *v.* 估计

15,000 people each year.

Some snakes can kill you by wrapping themselves around your body. They *squeeze* so hard that they cut off your air supply. That's what *pythons* do. These snakes are enormous. They can be up to 32 feet long. And they can weigh well over 300 pounds. You can find pythons in lots of places. They live in Australia, Africa, and Asia.

Like other snakes, pythons are deaf. They have good eyesight, but they'd have no trouble finding you even in the dark. That's because they could sense your body heat as you walked by. Pythons use their lips to pick up and locate the source of any body heat. Then they zero in on it. They *lunge* forward with their jaws stretched wide. A python could easily sink its sharp, backward-pointing teeth into your skin. Then it would wind its body around you. *Tighter* and

---

一些蛇可以缠绕住你的身体把你勒死。它们可以缠得很紧，以至于使人窒息。巨蟒就是这样做的。这些蛇很大。它们可能达到32英尺长。它们的体重可能达到300磅。你可以在许多地方找到巨蟒。它们栖息在澳大利亚、非洲和亚洲。

像其他蛇一样，巨蟒没有听觉。它们有很好的视力，但是它们即使在黑暗中也能毫不困难地发现你。那是因为当你经过时，它能感觉到你的体热。巨蟒使用嘴唇来感知，定位任何体热的来源。然后它们会瞄准这个体热。它们把嘴大大地张开然后向前扑去。巨蟒能够很容易地将尖利的、向后的牙刺入你的皮肤。然后它会把身体缠绕在你的身上。它会缠得越来越

---

squeeze *v.* 挤压

lunge *v.* 前冲

python *n.* 巨蟒

tight *adj.* 紧的

tighter it would wrap itself, squeezing its muscles as hard as it could. The result would be a death grip that would force all the air out of your body. It wouldn't take long for you to *suffocate* to death.

Pythons don't often go after human beings. Normally they feed on smaller animals. But every now and then, one breaks the *mold*. In 1979, for instance, a python waited in a grassy plain in South Africa. A teenage boy walked past, *herding* some cattle. All at once, the python struck. It moved like lightning. It drove its teeth through the boy's flesh. Then it *coiled* itself around his body. In minutes, the boy was dead.

Boa constrictors kill the same way as the python does. Other snakes, though, use a different method. They kill you by injecting poison into your body. This poison, called venom, is what a cobra

---

紧，尽量地收缩肌肉。其结果是致命的，它能够将所有的空气都挤出你的身体。不用多长时间就能使人窒息而死。

巨蟒不经常袭击人类。它们通常吃小一些的动物。但是时不时地，就会出现例外。比如1979年，一条巨蟒在南非的大草原上寻觅着。一个十几岁的男孩正好经过，他正在照看一群牲畜。突然之间，巨蟒袭击了。它出击的速度就好像是闪电一样。它的牙齿刺入了男孩的身体。然后马上把他缠住。几分钟之内，男孩就死了。

王蟒也采用与巨蟒相同的方式来捕杀。而其他一些蛇使用不同的方法。它们向你体内注射毒液来杀死你。这种毒素，叫作蛇毒，就是眼镜蛇

---

suffocate *v.* 窒息
herd *v.* 放牧

mold *n.* 模式
coil *v.* 盘绕

would use to kill you.

Cobras live in Asia and Africa. Like pythons, they are very big. Sometimes they grow to be about 18 feet long. The sight of a *cobra* in its attack *pose* is something you'll never forget. It lifts its head up from its coiled body. It stares at you with eyes that do not blink. The skin near its head puffs out, creating its famous "hood." When a cobra bites, *venom* flows from two fangs in its mouth. This venom quickly attacks your nerves. It can stop your heart. It can also *paralyze* your lungs.

Some cobras deliver their venom without biting. Three kinds of African cobras spit venom. They do this only when they feel threatened. But if you ever bother one—even accidentally—watch out! These cobras can hit targets from up to nine feet away. They

---

用来杀人用的东西。

　　眼镜蛇生活在亚洲和非洲。和巨蟒一样，它们也很大。有时它们能够达到18英尺长。眼镜蛇的攻击状态是令你永生难忘的。它从盘着的身体上竖起头。它的眼睛一眨不眨地盯着你。头附近的皮肤涨开，形成了眼镜蛇著名的"颈罩"。当眼镜蛇咬住时，蛇毒从口中的两颗牙中注入咬住的东西。这个蛇毒快速地袭击你的神经。它能够使心脏停止跳动。也会使你的肺部瘫痪。

　　还有一些眼镜蛇不需要咬住也能发出蛇毒。3种非洲眼镜蛇能够喷射蛇毒。它们只有当感觉受到威胁时才会这样做。但是如果你惹到了一条——即使是偶然的——小心！这些眼镜蛇能够准确地击中9英尺以外的

---

cobra *n.* 眼镜蛇　　　　　　　　　　　　　pose *n.* 姿势；姿态
venom *n.* 毒液　　　　　　　　　　　　　paralyze *v.* 使瘫痪

aim for the eyes. And they don't very often miss. If you get this venom in your eyes, you'll quickly go blind. Your sight may return after a while ... or you may be blinded for life.

Rattlesnakes have deadly venom too. Their venom can stop your heart and lungs. It can also cause bleeding inside your body. It can turn your *kidneys* and other organs to *mush*.

A rattlesnake will try to warn you if you come too close. It will shake the "rattle" on its tail. If you don't take the hint and move away, the rattlesnake may strike. Like the cobra, it has needle-sharp fangs. These teeth can cut right through leather shoes. One "rattler" proved that in 1988. A 12-year-old boy stepped on the snake near his Florida home. The snake's fangs *pierced* the boy's shoe and dug into his foot right near the anklebone. The boy almost died from the

---

东西。它们能够瞄准你的眼睛，而且经常十分准确。如果你的眼睛里面进了这种蛇毒，你很快就会失明。你的视力可能过一会能够恢复……或者你可能终身失明。

响尾蛇的蛇毒也是致命的。它们的蛇毒能够使心脏和肺瘫痪。它也能导致你体内出血。它能使你的肾或者其他器官融化成为糊糊。

如果你走得太近了，响尾蛇会试图警告你。它会摇晃尾部的发声器。如果你没有理会这个暗示，继续前进，响尾蛇可能会攻击。和眼镜蛇相近，它也有像针一样的牙齿，这些牙齿能够直接穿透皮革的鞋子。1988年一条响尾蛇证明了这一点。一个12岁的男孩在自己佛罗里达的家附近踩到了一条蛇，这条蛇的牙刺穿了男孩的皮鞋，刺入脚上部的踝骨附近。男

---

rattlesnake *n.* 响尾蛇

mush *n.* 糊状物

kidney *n.* 肾

pierce *v.* 刺穿

effects of the venom.

Rattlesnakes can make their move in the blink of an eye. In fact, the rattlesnake has the fastest attack time of any poisonous snake. In less than one second it can spring forward, bite, and draw back again. It moves so quickly that you may not see it. You will feel it, though. A rattlesnake's bite feels like hot *needles* being *jabbed* into your skin.

It takes about one teaspoon of rattlesnake venom to kill an adult human being. But it takes only a drop or two from a snake called the taipan. This snake lives in Australia. It may grow to 10 feet in *length*. It has orange eyes and a head shaped like a coffin. Taipans feed on mice, rats, and other small creatures. But they'll go after anything that *disturbs* them.

孩几乎死于蛇毒的感染。

响尾蛇能够在一眨眼的时间内采取行动。实际上，响尾蛇在各种毒蛇中的攻击时间最快。在一秒钟以内，它能够弹起，咬住，然后收回来。它的动作是如此之快以至于你可能没有看到。但是你能够感受到，响尾蛇咬住的动作感觉起来就好像是用烧红的针猛刺入你的皮肤。

一个汤匙的响尾蛇毒足够杀死一个成年人，但是一种叫作"泰潘蛇"的蛇毒一两滴就足够杀死一个人了。这种蛇生活在澳大利亚，可能长到10英尺长。它长着橙色的眼睛，头的形状就好像是棺材。泰潘蛇吃田鼠、仓鼠和其他的小动物。但是它们会袭击任何打扰了它们的人。

---

needle *n.* 针
length *n.* 长度

jab *v.* 刺
disturb *v.* 打扰

In 1991 Clive Brady was walking near Australia's Barron River. He came face to face with a taipan. Brady scrambled to get out of its way. But he wasn't fast enough. The snake *reared* up and bit his leg. Its jaws worked like a *jackhammer*, giving Brady seven quick bites. Then it let go and disappeared into the bushes.

Brady tried to walk toward help. But he didn't get far. Luckily, another man was down by the river that day. He rushed to get help for Brady. Nevertheless, by the time Brady arrived at the nearby hospital, he was in great pain. He couldn't stand. He was seeing double. His body was covered with *sweat*. His stomach was *clenched* tight. And his lungs were seizing up.

Doctors gave Brady medicine to fight the taipan's poison. But the venom had already caused bleeding inside his body. For hours

---

1991年，克里夫·布拉迪在澳大利亚的巴伦河附近散步。他与一条泰潘蛇面对面地相遇了，布拉迪慌乱地想逃走。但是跑得不够快。蛇抬起头，咬住了他的腿。它的下巴就像是个冲击钻头，短时间内咬了布拉迪7下。然后蛇松开了，然后消失在树丛里面。

布兰迪试图走出来寻求帮助。但是他未能跑多远。幸运的是，那一天，还有一个人也来到了小河旁边。他冲了上去帮助布兰迪。然而，当布兰迪到达附近的医院时，他已经出现了剧痛。他无法站立。他看到的东西已经出现了重影。他全身出汗。他的胃收缩得很紧，而且他的肺部也紧缩了。

医生马上给布兰迪对抗泰潘蛇蛇毒的药物。但是蛇毒已经导致了他的

---

rear *v.* 抬起（尤指头）　　　　jackhammer *n.* 手提钻
sweat *n.* 汗　　　　clench *v.* 紧闭(某物)；将(两物)紧压在一起

Brady bled from the fang marks on his leg. He also bled heavily from his gums. It took six hours for doctors to stop the bleeding. At last, they announced that Brady would live. He was very lucky. It could easily have gone the other way.

The medicine that saved Clive Brady is called antivenom. Doctors have come up with antivenom for all types of snakebites. But if you don't get it in time, it won't *do* you any *good*. The best thing to do, of course, is to *avoid* being bitten in the first place. But there are 300 kinds of poisonous snakes in the world. Add them to the snakes that can suffocate you, and you end up with a long list under the heading Do Not Disturb.

体内出血。几个小时以来，布兰迪腿上的牙印一直在出血。他的齿龈也严重出血。医生们用了6个小时来止住流血。最后他们宣布布兰迪得救了。他真是太幸运，太幸运了。这个情况很容易就能转向反面。

那种救了克里夫·布兰迪的药物叫作抗蛇毒血清。医生们已经研制出了对付所有蛇咬的抗蛇毒血清。但是如果你不能及时地得到注射，它不会有任何效果。当然最好是，一开始就不要被咬。但是世界上有300种毒蛇，再加上那些能够使你窒息的蛇，最终你在"不要惹"的题目下面要写上长长的一串名字。

---

do good 对……有好处；有用处　　　　　　　　　　　　avoid *v.* 避免

6

Rhinos VS. Humans

Not long ago, a tailor in Nepal needed some cloth. He *set off* for the market to buy it. The road took him through the Chitwan National Park. It was a path the tailor had walked many times before. He knew he had to be careful. Often he had seen or heard a rhinoceros in this area. The tailor knew that a *startled* rhino is

The largest of all rhinoceroses is the white rhinoceros. This beast can weigh more than three tons. By comparison, a small car weighs about one ton. Like a car, a rhino does a lot of damage when it hits something at high speed.

犀牛与人

在犀牛中体形最大的是白犀牛。这种动物的重量能够超过3吨。比较来说，小汽车的重量大约一吨。和车一样，当它高速奔跑时撞到什么东西造成的毁坏都是巨大的。

不久以前，尼泊尔的一名裁缝需要一些布料。他要去市场去买一些。这段公路通过奇特万国家公园，这也是裁缝以前经常走的道路。他知道他要很小心。他经常看到或者听说这个地区有犀牛。裁缝知道受惊的犀牛是

---

set off 出发   startled *adj.* 受惊的

a dangerous thing. If one decided to charge, it could easily *trample* him. In the past, the tailor had scared rhinos off by screaming. If that failed, he climbed a tree and waited until the animal went away.

On this morning, however, the tailor's luck ran out. He heard a rhino coming his way. It was a female with a young calf. The mother rhino must have *sensed* a threat, because all of a sudden she charged. The tailor leaped out of the way, grabbing an overhead tree branch. He tucked his legs up and wrapped them around the branch. He hung there, six feet off the ground, as the rhino rushed by. The animal's head was just high enough to hit him. She knocked him out of the tree. Turning around, the rhino trampled the tailor with her *hooves*. Then, using her sharp teeth, she ripped open the man's *belly*.

十分危险的。如果犀牛决定攻击，很容易就会把他踩到地上。以前，他曾经通过尖叫把犀牛吓跑过。如果这样做不起作用，他会爬上一棵树，直到那个畜生走远。

但是在今天上午，他就没有那么幸运了。他听到有一头犀牛向他这里走来了。那是一头雌性的犀牛，身边还有一头小犀牛。母犀牛一定是感到有危险，因为突然之间它发动了攻击。裁缝跳了起来抓住了头上的树枝。他卷起了腿，用它们钩住树枝。他悬挂在那里，当犀牛冲过时离地面有6英尺高。这个犀牛的头部刚好够高碰到了他。它把他从树上撞了下来。犀牛转过身子，用蹄子踩住了他。然后它用尖利的牙齿撕开了他的肚子。

---

trample *v.* 践踏
hoof *n.* 蹄

sense *v.* 感觉到
belly *n.* 肚子

We know about the tailor because he didn't die right away. His cries caught the ear of a man named Purney, who rushed to the tailor's aid. The tailor showed Purney his *wound* and told him what had happened. He asked Purney for a drink of water. Using his hat, Purney brought some water from a nearby stream. He then ran for help. But by the time he got back with some rescuers, the tailor was dead.

Purney told this tale to a nature writer named Fiona Sunquist. She retold it in her 1987 book *Tiger Moon*. Sunquist also wrote about her own close call. It was with a male rhino that had already killed two people. This beast was so famous that people had given him his own name-Triscar.

One day Sunquist hid in a tiny *grove* of trees. She wanted to

---

我们知道了这个裁缝的故事，因为他没有马上死掉。他的呼救声引起了一个叫作帕尼的人的注意，他冲向裁缝前去救援。裁缝给他看了伤口，讲述了发生的事情。他请帕尼给他一点水喝。帕尼使用他的帽子在附近的小溪中舀来了水。然后他跑出去寻找帮助。但是当他带着营救者回来时，裁缝已经死了。

帕尼把这个故事告诉了一个自然主题作家，叫作费欧娜·萨恩奎斯特。她在1987年的一本书《虎月》中重新讲述了这个故事。萨恩奎斯特也写了自己的危机时刻。那是同一头已经杀死了两个人的雄性犀牛之间的故事。这个畜生太出名了，以至于人们给它起了一个外号——"三条伤疤"。

一天，萨恩奎斯特藏在了一小丛树木里面，想要拍摄小犀牛在泥坑里

---

wound *n.* 伤口

grove *n.* 树丛

photograph a young rhino as it wallowed in a mud hole. Soon three adult rhinos also showed up. One was Triscar. Sunquist turned her camera on him. Although he did not see her, he headed toward the trees where she was hiding. "I stared in horror as his bulk filled, then overflowed, the *viewfinder*," she wrote. "He was six feet away, then two, and finally his nose touched the branches. All I could hear was the sound of his breath."

Triscar began eating some leaves inches from where Sunquist crouched. She thought she was going to die. Although rhinos have poor eyesight, they have a *keen* sense of smell. Sunquist figured the rhino would pick up her *scent* and kill her. But he didn't. The wind must have been blowing the other way. He never noticed her. After a while, he just moved away. Sunquist was left shaking with fear in a

---

面打滚的照片。很快三头成年犀牛也出现了。一头就是"三条伤疤"。萨恩奎斯特把照相机对准了它。虽然它无法看到她,但是它向着她藏身的树丛走来了。"我恐惧地发现它庞大的体形充满了镜头,然后冒出了镜头的视野,"她写道,"它在6英尺以外,然后2英尺,最后它的鼻子碰到了树枝。我能够听到它的呼吸声。"

"三条伤疤"开始吃离萨恩奎斯特藏身处仅仅几英寸地方的树叶,她以为她死定了。虽然犀牛的视觉很弱,但是它们的嗅觉很强。萨恩奎斯特觉得犀牛将会发觉她的气味,然后杀死她。但是它却没有这样做。一定是风向的关系。它一直就没有注意到她。过了一会,它就走开了。萨恩奎斯特在那里不断地发抖,流出了一滩的汗。

---

viewfinder *n.* 反光镜　　　　　　　　　　　　keen *adj.* 敏锐的
scent *n.* 气味

pool of sweat.

As the case of the tailor showed, Sunquist had reason to be afraid. Rhinos can and do attack human beings. This is especially true of a strong male or a female with her calf. These animals can be provoked by a slight sound or smell. It really does not take much. Sometimes they seem to charge for no reason at all. Unfortunately, people can get caught in the way. More human beings are killed by rhinos each year than by tigers or *leopards*.

If given the choice, rhinos would probably *stay away from* people altogether. After all, rhinos are not meat eaters. They have nothing to gain by attacking people. But the opposite is not true. People kill rhinos all the time. They go out of their way to do it. It's not because they need the meat. It's not because they fear for their lives. It's

---

正如裁缝事件所展示的情况，萨恩奎斯特有害怕的理由。犀牛能够并且确实在袭击人类。尤其是那些强壮的雄性和带有幼崽的雌性。一点声音或者气味都可能引起它们的攻击，的确不需要太多。有时看起来它们的攻击毫无原因，不幸的是，人们就这样遇到了麻烦。每年，犀牛杀死的人比老虎和美洲豹杀死的人还要多。

如果有机会，犀牛可能会远离人们。毕竟，犀牛不是食肉动物。它们攻击人类什么也得不到，但是相反情况却一直存在着。人们一直在猎杀犀牛，不是因为要吃它们的肉，也不是因为对自身生命的忧虑，而是因为他们要赚钱。

---

leopard *n.* 豹　　　　　　　　　　　　　　stay away from 远离

because they're trying to make money.

Poachers want rhino *horns*. Buyers will pay thousands of dollars for one. A horn can earn an African *poacher* enough money to live for a year. Some buyers turn the horns into knife handles for rich customers. Others use the horns to make expensive medicines.

With all the poaching, rhinos are fighting for their lives. Once they *roamed* Asia and Africa in great numbers. Today they are just barely hanging on. In Asia there are three kinds of rhinos. Put together, they add up to fewer than 2,000. Things are not much better in Africa. There are two kinds of African rhinos, the black and the white. Their numbers *add up to* fewer than 11,000.

To save the rhinos, officials have moved most of them to special parks. But that has not stopped all poachers. The money is so

---

偷猎者想要得到犀牛角。买主会出成千上万的美元来买一支。一支犀牛角可以使一名非洲偷猎者得到足够活一年的金钱。一些买主把犀牛角做成刀柄卖给有钱的顾客。还有人用犀牛角制作昂贵的药物。

在偷猎的威胁下，犀牛要保护它们的生命。它们曾在亚洲和非洲存在惊人的数目。但在今天它们却苦苦支撑着生存。在亚洲有3种犀牛，但是全部的加在一起也不超过2000头。在非洲也好不了太多，有两种非洲犀牛，黑犀牛和白犀牛，它们总共的数目不超过11,000头。

为了拯救犀牛，官员们将大多数的犀牛迁移到了特殊的公园里面，但是那也不能阻止所有的偷猎者。价格太高了，以至于一些人不惜铤而走

---

horn *n.* 角
roam *v.* 在……漫步

poacher *n.* 偷猎者
add up to 总计；总共

good that some are willing to take their chances. They sneak into the parks to kill the rhinos. Some African governments have struck back. In 1985 Zimbabwe launched Operation Stronghold. It was a *drastic* step. Park rangers could shoot poachers on sight. "Make no mistake," said one park warden. "We are fighting a very nasty bush war here, with no quarter given."

The ranger wasn't blowing smoke. He was dead serious. One morning two poachers shot a rhino in the Zambezi River Valley. The blast of their guns pierced the morning silence. Alerted, two park rangers moved in. They found the bloody trail of a dying black rhino. They also spotted two sets of footprints. These belonged to the poachers who had shot the rhino.

The rangers followed the trail. They *snuck up* on the poachers. As

---

险，他们偷偷潜入公园去杀死犀牛。一些非洲政府开始回击。1985年，津巴布韦开展了"堡垒行动"。这是一次强有力的行动。公园的巡查员可以击毙看到的偷猎者。"准确无误，"一名公园巡查员说，"我们正在进行一场非常残酷的丛林战争，毫无宽恕可言。"

巡查员不能制造烟火，要完全保持安静。一天早晨，两名偷猎者在赞比西河谷开枪击中了一头犀牛。他们的枪声划破了清晨的寂静。两名公园巡查员被惊醒了，他们开始行动。并发现了濒死犀牛的带血的脚印，他们也发现了两组人的脚印，它们是那些开枪的偷猎者的。

巡查员们跟踪脚印，悄悄地接近了偷猎者，当偷猎者蹲下身体去锯

---

drastic *adj.* 激烈的   sneak up 悄悄地靠近

the poachers bent to *cut off* the rhino's horn, the rangers closed to within 15 yards. Again, gunshots rang out. One of the poachers fell dead. The other tried to hide, but the rangers shot him, too.

At the end of two years, rangers had killed 13 poachers. "[The poachers] are the enemy," said one park official. "And we destroyed them."

Whose life is more precious—a human being's or a rhino's? It is sad that the question is even raised. But it doesn't have to be that way. Poachers wouldn't shoot rhinos if no one bought rhino-horn knives or medicines. Many nations have joined the fight to stop the trade of rhino products. Still, some people break the law. Rhino horns continue to be sold on the black market. That *spells* bad news for the few rhinos left in the wild.

断犀牛角时，巡查员们来到了15码以内。枪声再次响起，一名偷猎者被击毙。另一个试图藏起来，但是巡查员们将他也击毙了。

到两年年末时，巡查员们打死了13名偷猎者。"[偷猎者们]就是敌人，"一名公园的官员说，"我们消灭了他们。"

哪个生命更珍贵——是人的还是犀牛的？提出这个问题本身就令人感到悲哀。但是完全没有必要这个样子。如果没有人买犀牛角小刀或者犀牛角做的药，偷猎者就不会猎取犀牛。许多国家加入了与犀牛产品做斗争的行列。但是仍然有一些人违反法律，在黑市上犀牛角还在出售着。这为野生环境中为数不多的犀牛带来了不幸的消息。

---

cut off 切断

spell *v.* 招致

7

Danger —Rabid Animals!

Kelly Ahrendt did not feel well. She told her mother that her *knuckles* hurt and her left arm and shoulder *ached*. So on July 8, 1993, Margaret Ahrendt took her 11-year-old daughter to see a doctor. The doctor found a slight ear *infection* and a possible strep throat. But it was nothing serious. The doctor also thought Kelly might have pulled a

When an animal such as this raccoon has rabies, it can spread the disease to nearby human beings. Untreated rabies will quickly kill human victims if treatment isn't started right away.

狂犬病动物

当浣熊这样的动物得了狂犬病时，它能把狂犬病传染给附近的人们。如果受到狂犬病的感染，不马上处置，那就需要马上杀死人类感染者。

凯利·阿伦德感觉不好。她告诉她的母亲，她关节疼痛而且左胳膊和肩膀疼痛得厉害。这样在1993年7月8日，玛格丽特·阿伦德带着她11岁的女儿去看病。医生发现她有点耳道感染，有可能还有链球菌感染的喉炎，但是这并不严重。医生还认为凯利也可能是拉伤了肌肉。她是个女运

knuckle *n.* 关节
infection *n.* 感染

ache *v.* 疼痛

muscle. She was an athletic girl. She often did *cartwheels* outdoors on the family farm in New York. "It was no *big deal*," said Margaret. "[The doctor] said it was OK to go on vacation."

Everyone thought that Kelly would soon be her old self again. The next day the family set out on a camping trip in upstate New York, near Lake George. But Kelly didn't improve. In fact, she began to get sicker. She grew feverish. Her pains *intensified*. Then Kelly began having strange visions. "First she was crying, and then the crying stopped and she just started talking crazy," said her mother. "[Kelly screamed], 'The flies, get the flies off me!' And then she said she saw worms on her."

Margaret and her husband Richard were *desperate*. They took Kelly to three hospital emergency rooms. But doctors could do

---

动员。她经常在纽约的农场里面做翻筋斗的运动。"没什么大不了的，"玛格丽特说"[医生]说，假期去旅行没有问题。"

　　每个人认为凯利很快就痊愈。第二天整个家庭出发到纽约州北部乔治湖附近去野营。但是凯利没有好转。实际上，她变得更糟糕了。她开始出现发热，并且疼痛也加剧了。然后凯利开始出现奇怪的幻觉。"起初她开始哭，但是哭泣结束后，她开始像精神病一样讲话，"她的母亲说，"[凯利会尖叫]，'苍蝇，把苍蝇赶走！'然后她说，她看到了身上有虫子。"

　　玛格丽特和她的丈夫理查德绝望了。他们把凯利送到了三家医院的急

---

cartwheel *n.* 横翻筋斗　　　　　　　　　　big deal 了不起的事

intensify *v.* 增强　　　　　　　　　　　　desperate *adj.* 绝望的

nothing to stop her severe pain. Her muscles *twitched* violently. And her horrible visions grew worse. She was *disgusted* at the thought of her own hair. She even drew back whenever her parents came near. "I'm sorry," she told them. "I know I shouldn't be afraid of you, but I can't help it."

On July 11, Kelly Ahrendt died.

What caused this young girl's death? At first, the doctors had no idea. It was only later that the hard truth became clear. Laboratory tests showed that Kelly had died from rabies. She was the first person in New York to die from the disease since 1954.

Rabies is a deadly disease. Caused by a virus, it can strike most *mammals*—including humans. An animal with rabies passes it on to others by biting or *scratching*. Pets such as dogs and cats can have

---

救室，但是医生都对她严重的病痛无能为力。她的肌肉剧烈地抽搐着。她可怕的幻觉变得厉害了。她一想到自己的头发就感到恶心。甚至她的父母一靠近，她就会退缩。"抱歉，"她告诉他们，"我知道我不应该害怕你们，但是我无法控制这样的冲动。"

7月11日，凯利·阿伦德死了。

是什么导致了这个小女孩的死？起初医生们不知道。直到后来这个严重的问题才真正清晰了。通过试验表明凯利死于狂犬病。她是从1954年以来，在纽约第一个死于这种疾病的人。

狂犬病是一种致命的疾病。是由一种病毒引起的，它能够袭击大多数的哺乳动物——包括人。一种有狂犬病的动物通过咬或者抓把病毒传染给其他的人。一些宠物，如狗、猫都可能有狂犬病。实际上，在世界的大多

---

twitch *v.* 抽搐　　　　　　disgusted *adj.* 厌恶的；恶心的
mammal *n.* 哺乳动物　　　　scratch *v.* 抓

rabies. In fact, dogs are the greatest rabies threat in much of the world. Still, it is rare for dogs in the United States to have rabies. Here, most dogs and cats are *vaccinated* against the disease. So the real threat comes from wild animals. Raccoons, foxes, skunks, and other creatures can all catch the disease.

An animal with rabies—called a rabid animal—is not always easy to identify. It may look *tame* or just a bit sick. It might have trouble walking. You might see it do something *odd*. For instance, a night animal like a raccoon might be walking down the street in the middle of the day. If you ever run across such a creature, beware! It might be suffering from the most common *strain* of rabies, called the dumb strain. Victims of this strain often act slow-witted. Although your first impulse may be to help such an animal, don't do it. You can't save a

---

数地方，狗是最重要的狂犬病传染源。但是在美国狗却很少有狂犬病。在这里大部分的狗和猫都注射了疫苗。所以真正的威胁来自于野生的动物。浣熊、狐狸、臭鼬和其他的动物都很可能得这种疾病。

　　一只携带有狂犬病的动物——叫作狂犬病携带者——不容易发现。它看起来可能很老实或者像有点病，可能走路有些困难。你可能会发现它做什么奇怪的事情，比如一直在晚上活动的动物，如浣熊，可能在大白天走在公路上。如果你经过这样的动物，要小心！它可能正处在狂犬病最普通的阶段，叫作痴呆阶段。处在这个阶段的受害者经常表现出智能低下。虽然你的第一冲动可能是去帮助这个动物，但是千万不要那样做！你无法拯

---

vaccinate *v.* 给……注射疫苗
odd *adj.* 奇怪的

tame *adj.* 驯服的
strain *n.* 阶段

rabid animal, and you'll only put yourself at risk.

The other form of rabies is much easier to recognize. It is the *furious* strain. A dog with this type of rabies will foam at the mouth. It will howl constantly. It may *wander* for long distances. And it will attack for no reason at all. Any dog with furious rabies is as angry as an animal can get. That's where the expression mad dog comes from.

Rabies in humans is difficult to *diagnose*. That's because the virus doesn't travel through the blood stream. If it did, it would show up in a blood test. Instead, rabies spreads through the nerve cells. The virus slowly works its way up to the brain. While this is happening, the victim shows no signs of the disease. This period can last anywhere from ten days to seven months. The time *frame* depends

---

救一只得了狂犬病的动物，你只能把你自己陷入危险之中。

另一种狂犬病很好辨认。那就是狂躁阶段。一条得了这种病的狗会口吐白沫，它会经常鬼哭狼嚎，它会长时间地逛来逛去，它可能毫无理由进行攻击。任何狗如果得了狂犬病就会像任何其他暴怒的动物那样。这就是"疯狗"这个词的来历。

人体中的狂犬病很难作出诊断。那是因为这种病毒不通过血液传播。如果是通过血液传播，在血液检查中也能够显示出来。但是狂犬病是通过神经细胞扩散。狂犬病毒缓慢地向大脑移动。当这个过程处于扩散期时，受害者没有疾病的标志。这个过程可能持续阶段很长，从10天到7个月。时间表完全取决于病毒在哪里进入身体。

---

furious *adj.* 狂怒的

diagnose *v.* 诊断

wander *v.* 闲逛

frame *n.* 框架

on where the virus entered the body.

When rabies finally reaches the brain, symptoms appear. These include crazy fears, foaming at the mouth, and muscle *spasms*. By this time, it's too late for treatment. The disease at this point is always *fatal*. So even if the doctors had *figured out* what was wrong with Kelly Ahrendt, they couldn't have saved her. Once symptoms appear, death follows quickly. Most victims, like Kelly, die within a week.

The Ahrendts had known all about the threat of rabies. They knew that rabid raccoons had recently appeared in New York. Margaret had even read an article about a rabid cat to her seven children. She warned the children not to touch raccoons or other wild animals. "Kelly knew—all the kids knew—about the animals," Margaret said.

当病毒最终到达大脑时，症状开始出现。这包括疯狂地恐惧，口中出现白沫，肌肉痉挛。到此时，治疗已经来不及了。这个阶段的疾病经常是致命的。所以即使医生们已经看出凯利·阿伦德的病，他们也无法挽救她。一旦症状出现了，死亡就接踵而至。大部分的受害者和凯利一样，在一个星期内死亡。

阿伦德一家已经完全知道了狂犬病的威胁。他们知道带有狂犬病的浣熊在纽约出现。甚至玛格丽特向她的7个孩子读了一篇文章，上面写了带有狂犬病的猫的情况。她警告孩子们不要碰浣熊和其他的野生动物。"凯利知道——所有的孩子们都知道——动物的情况，"玛格丽特说。"如果

---

spasm *n.* 痉挛   fatal *adj.* 致命的
figure out 想出；考虑出

"If they saw a raccoon, they'd usually all come screaming into the house."

So how did Kelly get the disease? At first, it was a total mystery. The Ahrendts had some animals on their farm. They had two cats, a dog, two horses, three rabbits, and some ducks and chickens. But none of these animals were rabid. If one had been, it would have died before Kelly did. And, given her mother's firm warning, it was not likely that Kelly got close enough to be bitten by a rabid raccoon.

In late August doctors finally solved the mystery. More lab tests showed that Kelly had gotten rabies from a bat. It turned out that bats lived in the *attic* of the family home. But no one knew exactly how Kelly had come into *contact* with the bats. Did one of them bite or scratch her? Maybe not. A bite or a scratch isn't always

---

他们见到浣熊，他们经常是都尖叫着跑回屋子。"

凯利是怎样得了这个疾病的呢？刚开始这完全是个谜。阿伦德在农场里面养了一些动物。他们有两只猫、一条狗、两匹马、三只兔子和一些鸡鸭。但是这些动物都没有狂犬病。如果有狂犬病它就会在凯利死前死去，而且既然她母亲已经严肃地警告过，凯利也不太可能能够走得太近让带有狂犬病的浣熊咬到。

在8月下旬，医生们终于解决了这个问题。更多的试验证明凯利是从蝙蝠那里得到的病毒。原来家里房子阁楼里面有蝙蝠。但是没有人知道凯利怎么和蝙蝠联系在了一起。是不是其中的一只咬到或者抓伤了她呢？也许不是。不用咬伤或者抓伤。携带狂犬病毒的蝙蝠可以通过空气来传播这

---

attic *n.* 阁楼

contact *n.* 联系

necessary. It is possible for bats with rabies to send the virus through the air. Two people are known to have picked up rabies this way. They got it just by breathing the air in caves filled with rabid bats.

People infected with rabies don't have to die. But steps must be taken before the symptoms start. So if you ever *suspect* you've been exposed to rabies, see a doctor—quickly! There is a cure. It was developed by Louis Pasteur in 1885. For a long time, this cure involved a *grim* treatment. Victims had to have a series of 14 to 21 injections in the stomach. Today the cure is more *bearable*. It consists of five shots in the arm. That treatment still may sound pretty painful. But when you think of the *alternative*, it's not hard to roll up your sleeve and face the needle.

种病毒。已经有两个人通过这种方式得了狂犬病。他们只是吸入了布满狂犬病毒山洞里面的空气得病的。

感染了狂犬病的人不是一定要死，但是在症状出现前，必须经过那些阶段。所以如果你觉得你曾经有过感染狂犬病的危险，要马上去看医生！还是有治愈的可能的。这是1885年路易斯·帕斯特尔发明的方法。长期以来，这种方法涉及严格的治疗方法。受害者要进行一系列的14至21次在腹部的注射。今天的方法更加容易接受，它包括在胳膊上的5次注射。这个治疗听起来很疼痛，但是你想象一下另外一种可能，就很容易卷起衣服面对针头了。

---

suspect *v.* 怀疑；猜想
bearable *adj.* 可忍受的

grim *adj.* 冷酷的；残忍的
alternative *n.* 二中择一

8

Night Killers

They come out at night. Flying just three feet over the ground, they are constantly on the lookout for blood. Their four white fangs *glisten* in the light of the moon. They hunt by sound and by smell. As they *swoop* past, they make an angry *sputtering* noise. These night killers are *vampire* bats. You don't want to be around

Like the mythical creature it was named for, the vampire bat drinks its victims' blood. This bat usually ignores humans, preferring to drink the blood of large animals. But in a pinch, it looks for blood wherever it can find it.

夜半杀手

就和它得到的那个神秘的名字一样，吸血鬼蝙蝠吸受害者的血。这种蝙蝠经常不袭击人而是喝一些大型动物的血。但是在紧要关头，他们也会饥不择食。

它们在晚上行动。就在地面上方3英尺的高度飞行，它们总是在寻找血源。它们那四个雪白的牙齿在月光下闪闪发光。它们通过声音和气味来打猎，当它们发动突然袭击时，它们会发出愤怒的噼啪声。它们就是夜晚杀手吸血鬼蝙蝠。当它们出来觅食时，你可不会喜欢在附近出现。

glisten *v.* 闪光

sputter *v.* 发噼啪声

swoop *v.* 突然袭击

vampire *n.* 吸血鬼

when they're out looking for a meal.

Vampire bats live in Central America and parts of Mexico. They are not very big. Most weigh only about one ounce. Their bodies are just three inches long, or the size of a human thumb. Even with their wings stretched out, they are only eight inches wide. Still, these tiny creatures can kill a cow. Just ask Cesar Murillo, a cattle rancher in Mexico. In 1995 vampire bats killed more than 50 cows in his *herd*. Using heat *sensors* in the nose, vampire bats find a *vein* close to the surface of the victim's skin. Legend says they suck the blood out of their victim. But that isn't true. Instead, they use their sharp teeth to cut the flesh. Often they make their *incision* behind an ear, an elbow, or a hoof. Then they lick the blood from the open wound. Vampire bats can drink their own body weight in warm blood at one meal.

吸血鬼蝙蝠生活在中美洲和墨西哥的部分地区。它们并不大,大部分的重量只有一盎司。它们的身体只有3英寸长,或者人的大拇手指大小。即使它们的翅膀完全展开,也仅有8英寸宽。但是这些小东西能够杀死牛。只要问一问西撒尔·姆里罗就可以了,他是墨西哥的一个养牛的农场主。1995年,吸血鬼蝙蝠杀死了他的牛群的五十多头牛。吸血鬼蝙蝠使用鼻子里面的热感应器,找到受害者皮肤附近的血管。传说中它们把血吸出来,但是这并不正确。实际上,它们是使用尖利的牙齿切开肉。它们经常的切口部位是耳朵、肘部、蹄子等。然后它们从伤口处舐血喝。吸血鬼蝙蝠可以一次喝上与它身体重量相同的血,那需要一会的时间。有时它们

---

herd *n.* 兽群
vein *n.* 血管

sensor *n.* 传感器
incision *n.* 切口

That can take a while. Sometimes their *gory* feast will last as long as 20 minutes.

Because vampire bats come out at night, their victims are usually asleep at the time of the attack. The bats have a special chemical in their *saliva*. It *numbs* the victim's skin. That way, they can sink their teeth in without waking the victim. The bats use a second chemical to keep the blood from drying up while they eat.

The real trouble with these nasty creatures isn't the blood they take away. It's the diseases they leave behind. Vampire bats carry several deadly diseases, including rabies. That's how they killed Cesar Murillo's cows. As they *lapped up* the cows' blood, they infected the cows with rabies.

Within a few days, the cows began to act very strange. Murillo

---

的血淋淋的大餐会持续20分钟。

因为吸血鬼蝙蝠在晚上出动，所以在袭击时它们的受害者经常是熟睡的。这种蝙蝠的唾液里面有一种特殊的化学物。它会使受害者的皮肤麻木。这样，它们可以在不影响受害者睡眠的情况下将它们的牙齿切入。这种蝙蝠使用另一种化学物质使血不会在它们用餐时凝固。

这种肮脏的动物的真正问题不是它们吸走的血，而是它们留下的疾病。吸血鬼蝙蝠携带着一些致命的疾病，包括狂犬病。那才是真正杀死西撒尔·姆里罗母牛的东西。当它们舔母牛的血时，它们把母牛感染了狂犬病。

在几天内，母牛们开始行为变异。姆里罗描述了这种病如何影响到了

---

gory *adj.* 血淋淋的
numb *v.* 使麻痹

saliva *n.* 唾液
lap up 舔食

described how the disease affects cows. "They start to lose their ability to walk," he said. "Their back legs *buckle* when they try to stand. Then they start trying to crawl. They get this desperate look in their eyes. A short time later, they die."

As bad as the situation was for Murillo, it was much worse for people in Nicaragua. There, in 1999, vampire bats started to attack humans. One morning, the parents of two young girls woke up to find vampire bats drinking the blood of their sleeping daughters. In another case, a small girl died from rabies after being attacked by vampire bats. In all, he bats attacked at least 22 people.

These attacks were most unusual. Vampire bats prefer the blood of large birds, cows, horses, and pigs. They live in deep caves or old wells. So normally they don't go near humans. But in 1998 *Hurricane*

母牛，"它们开始失去行走的能力，"他说，"当它们想站起来时，后腿相互扣住，无法站立，然后它们就试图爬行，它们的眼中是绝望的神情。用不了多长时间，它们就死了。"

姆里罗的情形十分糟糕，在尼加拉瓜的人遇到的情况要更加糟糕。1999年在那里吸血鬼蝙蝠开始攻击人类。一天早晨，一对两个女孩的父母醒来时发现吸血鬼蝙蝠正在吸他们熟睡的女儿们的血。在另一个事件中，一个小女孩在受到吸血鬼蝙蝠的攻击后死于狂犬病。吸血鬼蝙蝠总共袭击了至少22个人。

这些攻击是很反常的。吸血鬼蝙蝠喜欢大型鸟类、牛、马和猪的血。它们生活在很深的山洞和古老的井里面。所以正常情况下，它们距离人很远。但

---

buckle *v.* 扣住   hurricane *n.* 飓风

Mitch struck Nicaragua. That storm brought record-breaking rains. Many caves and wells were flooded. Bats were forced out of their *rural* homes and into places where people lived. (Heavy rains had also helped *trigger* the outbreak of bat attacks on cows in Mexico.)

In one Nicaraguan town, people had to fight the bats for several months. "Every night they're after us," said one farmer. "The cows, the horses, and us too."

Many people in the town *rubbed* garlic on their animals. Aris Mejia explained why. Mejia was one of a dozen bat killers hired by the government. "The bats just don't like the *odor* [of garlic]," he said. "[But] it only lasts one night. If you don't put fresh garlic on the animals the next night, the bats come back."

Mejia found a more permanent solution. His job was to kill as

是1998年米奇飓风袭击了尼加拉瓜。这次风暴导致了创纪录的暴雨。许多山洞和井里面都洪水泛滥。蝙蝠被迫离开了它们在乡村的家，它们来到了人类居住的地方。（大暴雨也导致了蝙蝠大量袭击墨西哥的牛。）

在尼加拉瓜的一个小镇，人们要用几个月的时间与蝙蝠作斗争。"每个晚上它们都在袭击我们，"一个农民说，"袭击牛、马还有我们。"

在城镇里面的许多人在它们的牲畜身上擦大蒜。艾力斯·麦加解释了它的原因。麦加是政府雇佣的12名捕杀蝙蝠的人之一。"蝙蝠就是不喜欢[大蒜的]气味，"他说，"[但是]这只是一个晚上有效，如果你第二天没有把新鲜的大蒜涂在牲畜身体上，蝙蝠就会再回来。"

麦加也发现了更为固定的解决方案。他的工作是尽可能多地捕杀吸血

rural *adj.* 乡村的
rub *v.* 擦

trigger *v.* 引发；引起
odor *n.* 味

many vampire bats as he could. He started hunting each night as soon as the sun went down. *Slaying* bats wasn't a nice job. "It's kind of strange work, and not everyone in Nicaragua likes to do it," said Mejia. "You can always tell us by our scars." One vampire bat left an ugly scar on his left hand. It bit right through the thick gloves he was wearing.

Mejia didn't hunt vampire bats with a gun. He didn't try to expose them to the sunlight. And he didn't try to drive a *stake* through their hearts. Those weapons are used only in fiction when the *villain* is a human vampire. Instead, Mejia went after the bats with a net. If he could find where they lived, he would cover the entrance with his net. He could then *trap* the bats when they tried to come out.

If he couldn't find the bats' homes, Mejia used a different

鬼蝙蝠。每天晚上一到夜幕降临，他就开始捕杀蝙蝠。杀蝙蝠可不是一个好活。"这是一种奇怪的工作，而且并不是所有尼加拉瓜的人都喜欢这个工作，"麦加说，"你可以从我们的伤疤上看出我们的身份。"一只吸血鬼蝙蝠在他的左手上留下了一条丑陋的疤痕。它一下子就咬穿了他戴着的厚手套。

麦加不使用枪支来捕猎吸血鬼蝙蝠。他不想在太阳下展示出它们，他也不想在它们的心脏上穿上一个木桩。这些武器只是在小说中对付人的吸血鬼才使用。实际上麦加用一张网来追捕蝙蝠。如果他发现它们在哪里生活，他就会用网把入口罩住。这样当它们试图出来时，他就可以把它们套住。

如果麦加不能找到它们的窝，他就使用一种不同的方法。他会让一

---

slay *v.* 杀死
villain *n.* 坏人；恶棍

stake *n.* 桩
trap *v.* 使……陷入困境

approach. He would have a farmer put all his animals in one *corral*. In this way, the cows, horses, and pigs would serve as *bait*. Then Mejia would wait. He knew the vampire bats would find them in a few nights. When they did, he would be waiting for them with his net.

After catching a bat, Mejia would *smear* it with poison and then let it go. The poison was strong enough to kill the bat, but it acted slowly. That was the plan. The released bat would fly back to its home. Other bats in the colony would then lick the poisoned bat in an attempt to clean it. Or sometimes the bats would fight and bite the poisoned bat. Either way, the others would swallow the poison. Within a few days all the bats in that colony would be dead. "For every bat we capture," said Mejia, "we can kill up to 10 or 15."

个农民把他所有的牲畜都关进一个畜栏。这样，牛、马、猪就可以作为诱饵。然后，麦加会等待。他知道吸血鬼蝙蝠在几个夜晚就能够找到它们。如果它们找来了，他就用网来等待它们。

　　一旦抓住一只蝙蝠，麦加就会用毒药涂在它的身上，然后就把它放走。这个毒药足够厉害能够杀死蝙蝠，但是起作用的时间很缓慢。那是一个计划。这只放走的蝙蝠就会飞回它的巢穴。巢穴中的其他蝙蝠会把这个蝙蝠舔干净。或者其他蝙蝠会与那只蝙蝠打架或者咬它。无论怎样，另外的蝙蝠也会吞下毒药。几天之内，那个巢穴里面的蝙蝠都会死亡。"我们抓住一只蝙蝠，就会杀死累积到10或15只。"

---

approach *n.* 方法

bait *n.* 诱饵

corral *n.* 畜栏

smear *v.* 涂上

To many people, poisoning vampire bats sounds cruel. After all, most of the time these tiny creatures are not a big *threat*. They stay away from humans and attack only a few farm animals. But if heavy rains force the bats to look for food in other places, they become a huge problem. No one wants to wake up to find a vampire bat licking blood from his or her toes. When bats start to attack humans, bat killers such as Aris Mejia are in big *demand*.

对于许多人来说，毒药杀死蝙蝠听起来残酷一些。毕竟大部分的时间这种小动物不是个很大的威胁。它们远离人类，只是攻击一些牲畜。但是暴雨使蝙蝠要在其他地方寻找食物的话，它们就成为一个大问题。没有人希望醒来时发现吸血鬼蝙蝠在舔他脚趾上面的血。当蝙蝠开始攻击人类时，就像艾力斯·麦加这样的蝙蝠捕杀者大大地需要。

---

threat *n.* 威胁　　　　　　　　　　　　　　　demand *n.* 需要

9

The Man-Eating Komodo Dragon

Imagine this scene. You're walking through the Indonesian jungle with some friends. After a while, you become tired and decide to rest a bit. You sit down on a log, telling your friends to keep going. You'll *catch up with* them later. As you begin to relax, you suddenly realize that you're not alone. Your blood runs cold. When you

Here, four full-grown Komodo dragons fight over a chunk of goat meat. Given the chance, any of the four would take all the meat for itself. And if there were not meat available, it would attack its fellows.

食人巨蜥

　　这里四条成年的巨蜥正在争夺一大块山羊肉。如果有机会其中的任何一条都可以独自吃掉所有的肉。而且如果没有肉，它们就会攻击它们的同伴。

　　想象一下这个景象。你在印度尼西亚的丛林中和朋友们一起行走。过了一会，你感到累了，决定休息片刻。你坐在一根圆木上面告诉你的朋友们继续走。你过一会赶上他们。当你开始休息一会时，你突然感到好像还有什么东西。你的血液突然凝固了。你一转身，就发现你和一条10英尺

catch up with　追上；赶上

MCGRAW-HILL

turn around, you find yourself face to face with a 10-foot Komodo dragon rapidly *flicking* its tongue in and out. Say hello to the world's largest lizard. But do it fast. This dragon isn't here to talk.

Luckily for you, you're not really sitting on that log. But a real person once did sit on a similar log. He was a Swiss tourist visiting the island nation of Indonesia. He grew tired of hiking and sent his friends on ahead. Later, when the tourist didn't show up, his friends went looking for him. All they found was his camera *case* and a bloody shirt. Everything else had been eaten by a hungry Komodo dragon.

Then there is the story of a father and his two adult sons. They went into the Indonesian jungle to cut some wood. The *tropical* heat tired them out. And the work was *tedious*. So the men were not

---

长的巨蜥正好面对面，它正在迅速地抽动着舌头，向世界上最大地蜥蜴问好，但是动作要快。巨蜥来到这里可不是来聊天的。

你很幸运，你没有真的坐在那块原木上面。但是真的曾经有人坐到了相似的原木上面。他是一名瑞士的旅行者，他到岛国印度尼西亚来旅行。他走得累了，让朋友们先走。后来旅行者没有出现，他的朋友们回来寻找他。他们所找到的就是他的照相机盒和一件满是鲜血的衬衫。其他的部分都被一只饥饿的巨蜥吃光了。

这里还有一个父亲和他的两个儿子的故事。它们来到印度尼西亚的丛林里面砍一些木头。热带的炎热很快就使他们筋疲力尽，而且工作又是枯燥的。所以他们并不是很警觉。直到一切都太晚的时候，他们才注意到

---

flick *v.* 快而轻地移动　　　　　　　　case *n.* 盒子
tropical *adj.* 热带的　　　　　　　　　tedious *adj.* 乏味的；枯燥的

particularly alert. They didn't notice the Komodo dragon sneaking up on them until it was too late. The lizard *leapt* at the three men. They jumped out of the way and began to run for their lives. But one of the sons got caught in a low-hanging *vine*. In a flash, the Komodo dragon seized him and bit off a huge chunk of his back. The father and the other son raced back and beat the lizard off. But it was too late. The son who had been attacked bled to death within an hour.

You may be relieved to learn that your chances of running into a Komodo dragon are pretty slim. You can find these lizards at some large zoos. Other than in these zoos, they live on only a few small islands in Indonesia. They get their name from one of these islands, Komodo. If you should happen to visit these islands, take care. *Heed* the warning signs along jungle paths. Pay attention when the signs

---

一只巨蜥向他们爬了上来。巨蜥向3个人扑了过去。他们跳了起来开始逃命。但是一个儿子被低垂的藤条缠住了。那一瞬间，巨蜥抓住了他，咬掉了他后背的一大块肉。父亲和另一个儿子又赶快冲了回来把巨蜥打跑。但是一切都太晚了。这个儿子受到攻击内一小时因为失血过多致死。

你可能会认为遇到这种巨蜥的可能性很小。你可以在一些大公园见到这种巨蜥。除了这些公园外，它们只是在印度尼西亚的一些小岛上生存。它们的名字也是来自于一个小岛的名字："科摩多"。如果你碰巧到这些小岛去游览可一定要小心。要注意丛林道路两旁的警示牌。注意写着"危

---

leap *v.* 跳跃   vine *n.* 藤
heed *v.* 注意

say Dangerous Area or WATCH OUT: Komodo Crossing. Otherwise, you might end up in the opening paragraph of a story like this.

The Komodo dragon certainly looks the part of a killer. It has *scaly* skin, a yellow forked tongue, sharp teeth, and curved claws. It's also huge! Most Komodos are about seven feet long. A few grow to be 10 feet. Many weigh 200 pounds. Some are even bigger than that. The biggest ones probably come close to 500 pounds. It's hard to be *precise*, though—no one has volunteered to weigh them!

Komodo dragons are *predators*. They feed off the flesh of the animals they kill. Often they attack small creatures such as rats, goats, hens, monkeys, and pigs. But sometimes they move up to larger *prey*. One of their top targets is deer. A few Komodos have killed animals as large as a horse or a water buffalo.

险地区"或者"小心：巨蜥出没"的字样。否则你可能会面对着文章开头那样的结局。

科摩多巨蜥看起来是不折不扣的杀手形象。它们的皮肤上有鳞片，有一条黄色分叉的舌头、尖利的牙齿和弯曲的爪子，而且它们体形庞大！大多数的科摩多巨蜥有7英尺长，一些能够长到10英尺长，许多的重量达到200磅，还有一些甚至比这还要大，最大的能够达到500磅。很难精确地说——没有人愿意去称一称它们！

科摩多巨蜥是食肉动物。它们靠捕杀动物，吃掉它们生活。它们经常攻击小动物，如：老鼠、山羊、鸡、猴子和猪。但是有时他们也去攻击大一些的猎物。它们的顶级目标是鹿。一些科摩多巨蜥甚至杀死了像马、水牛这样的动物。

---

scaly *adj.* 有鳞的
predator *n.* 食肉动物

precise *adj.* 精确的
prey *n.* 猎物

Komodos have a simple system for killing big animals. It's the same method that was used on the Indonesian woodcutter. The Komodo *lunges* at its prey with lightning speed. It takes a huge bite out of the victim's stomach or backside. Then it waits patiently while the poor victim bleeds to death.

Komodo dragons always hunt alone. They don't seem to trust each other. And they have reason to be *suspicious*. If a Komodo does not find anything else to eat, it is perfectly willing to feast on its fellow Komodos.

Komodo dragons are skillful killers. They are not fast enough, however, to run down most of their prey. They can run up to 11 miles an hour, but only for a short *stretch*. So they *ambush* their prey from behind. At times they also take to the water in search of

---

　　科摩多巨蜥的捕杀招数很一致，和在印度尼西亚伐木者身上使用的方法一样。科摩多巨蜥以闪电的速度冲向猎物。在受害者的腹部或者背部撕下一大块肉，然后它耐心地等待可怜的受害者失血过多而死。科摩多巨蜥经常单独捕猎。看起来它们好像并不相互信任，它们有足够的原因来怀疑。如果科摩多巨蜥没有找到什么吃的，它是很愿意把同伴当成一顿大餐的。

　　科摩多巨蜥是很讲究技巧的杀手。它们跑得不够快，追不上它们的大多数猎物。它们可以达到每小时11英里的速度，但只是一小段的时间。所以它们从背后偷袭猎物。有时它们也到水里去寻找猎物。科摩多巨蜥水性

---

lunge *v.* 猛冲；猛扑
stretch *n.* 连续的一段时间

suspicious *adj.* 可疑的
ambush *v.* 埋伏；伏击

food. Komodos are fine swimmers. They have no trouble diving or swimming through strong ocean *currents*.

Komodo dragons are terribly smart. They plan some of their meals far in advance. They do this by keeping watch on *pregnant* goats and horses. Komodos like to be around just after these creatures give birth. A helpless mother and her newborn babies make a great meal.

Big Komodo dragons are also *scavengers*. They will eat the meat of animals they didn't kill. And it's not just animal meat they crave. Komodos have been found digging in cemeteries. They were trying to get at human *corpses* that had been buried there.

Clearly, Komodos will eat just about any kind of flesh they can find. They don't care if it is fresh or rotten. In fact, the smellier and

---

很好，在强有力的海流中它们也可以随意地进行潜水和游泳。

科摩多巨蜥很聪明。它们很早就会计划它们的大餐。它们一直在观察怀孕的山羊和马，当这些动物生产时，它们最喜欢到来。一个无助的母亲和它新生下来的孩子们是很好的一顿大餐。

大型的科摩多巨蜥也是食腐动物。它们会吃掉不是它们杀死的动物的尸体，而且它们不仅是渴求动物的尸体。曾经有人发现科摩多巨蜥在墓地里面挖掘，它们试图找到埋在那里的尸体。

很明显，科摩多巨蜥将吃掉它们能够找到的任何肉。它们不在意是新鲜的还是腐烂的。实际上，越有气味，越腐烂越好，有强烈气味的物体使

---

current *n.* 涌流

scavenger *n.* 食腐动物

pregnant *adj.* 怀孕的

corpse *n.* 尸体

more rotten the meat, the better. A strong odor just makes the food easier to find. A Komodo *sniffs* out rotting meat with its tongue. This tongue can detect a meal from as far away as five miles. The tongue also lets you know if the lizard considers you a good meal. The faster a Komodo flicks its tongue in and out, the tastier it thinks you will be.

Once a Komodo dragon finds food, it isn't shy about eating it. It will *chow* down its meal as fast as possible. There is a reason for the bad manners. Every Komodo wants to prevent other Komodos from stealing its goat or pig or deer. An average Komodo can bite off the *hindquarter* of a goat in one *gulp*. A 110-pound Komodo once ate a 68-pound pig in 17 minutes. Komodos can eat up to 80 percent of their body weight in one meal. If you weighed 100 pounds, you

---

寻找起来更加容易。科摩多巨蜥通过它的舌头闻出烂肉的位置。它们的舌头可以探到五英里外的食物。舌头会展示出巨蜥是否把你当作美味来看，科摩多巨蜥的舌头伸缩得越快，它就越觉得你好吃。

当科摩多巨蜥找到食物时，它们吃起来可不怎么矜持，它们会狼吞虎咽地把食物尽快地吞下去。这个不礼貌的行为是有其原因的。每条巨蜥都要防止其他的巨蜥偷走它的山羊、猪或者鹿。一条普通的巨蜥能够一口咬掉一只山羊的后腿。一次，一条110磅重的科摩多巨蜥在17分钟内吃掉了一头68磅重的猪。科摩多巨蜥能够在一顿饭中吃掉自己体重80%的食物。

---

sniff *v.* 闻

hindquarter *n.* 后腿

chow *v.* 吃

gulp *n.* 一大口；吞咽

would have to eat 320 quarter-pound burgers to match that record.

And Komodo dragons don't waste anything. They will swallow a goat's head, including its horns and teeth. They will eat a *porcupine*, *quills* and all. The *hooves* of a horse are no problem, either. It's hard to think of any animal that is a more efficient eater.

The habits of a Komodo dragon might seem *disgusting* to you. You would not be alone in that opinion. But the Komodo dragon is a marvel of nature. It knows what it wants, and it knows how to get it. All you have to do is be sure that what it wants isn't you!

如果你的体重是100磅，你要吃掉320个大号汉堡才能与这个记录相比。

而且科摩多巨蜥一点也不剩。它会把山羊的头，包括角和牙齿都吞下去。在吃豪猪时，它会把刺也吃下去。马的蹄子当然更不是问题。很难想象什么动物能比它更有效率。

科摩多巨蜥的习惯可能对于你来说很恶心。按照这个观点，你可不要一个人行动。但是科摩多巨蜥是大自然的一个奇迹。它知道它想要什么，而且知道如何得到它。你所要做的就是弄清楚，它需要的不是你！

---

porcupine *n.* 豪猪   quill *n.* （豪猪的长而硬的）刺

hoof *n.* 蹄   disgusting *adj.* 令人厌恶的

10

Elephant on the Rampage

Kathy Lawler thought it sounded like *fun*. Her children, eight-year-old Lauren and three-year-old C. J. , couldn't wait to do it. So Lawler paid for them all to have a ride on a *circus* elephant. The Lawlers hoped to get a nice, gentle ride. Instead they got the ride of their lives.

It was almost 5 o'clock in the

Elephants are usually intelligent, gentle, and sociable animals. However, an elephant that is mistreated or kept in a small space can lose its patient and agreeable nature. Then watch out!

暴怒的大象

大象经常是聪明、温顺而且团队精神很强的动物。但是一头受到虐待或者关在小地方的大象会失去它的耐心和对自然平和的心态。那么要小心！

凯西·劳拉觉得听起来很有趣。她的孩子们忍不住想去玩，他们是8岁的劳林和3岁的C. J. 。所以劳拉付款让他们3个人一起骑上马戏团的大象。劳拉一家希望得到温顺的美好驾乘感受，但是他们却冒了生命的危险。

1992年2月1日，大约是在晚上5点左右。美国大马戏团即将在佛罗里

---

fun *n.* 有趣的事　　　　　　　　　　　　circus *n.* 马戏团

evening on February 1, 1992. The Great American Circus was about to start in Palm Bay, Florida. First, though, people in the crowd could take elephant rides. Lawler and her children climbed onto an Indian elephant named Kelly. They sat in a metal basket on her back. Three other children also climbed on.

Kelly was a circus pro. She had been giving rides for more than 10 years. She always moved slowly, walking next to a metal fence inside the ring. Lawler thought Kelly looked very tame. Her *stride* seemed firm and steady. As the ride began, C. J. and the other children screamed with delight.

Then it happened. "About two-thirds of the way around the ring, Kelly smashed into [the fence]," Lawler later recalled. "And I thought, 'Well, she's a little *testy* today. I'll be glad when this ride is over.'" Lawler didn't know it, but the "ride" was just beginning.

达的棕榈海岸进行表演。首先人群中的人们可以骑大象。劳拉和她的孩子们爬上了一头叫作凯利的印度大象上。她们坐在大象后背的一个金属篮子里面。另外的3个孩子也爬了进来。

凯利是马戏团的老手了。它已经被人骑了10年了。它总是缓慢地移动，在圈里面的金属围栏旁边行走。劳拉觉得凯利看起来十分温顺，它的脚步看起来坚实稳重。当开始行走时，C. J. 和其他的孩子都高兴地叫了起来。

然后就发生了可怕的一幕。"当圈转到了三分之二的地方时，凯利撞到了[围栏]，"后来劳拉回忆道，"我想，好啊，它今天想要玩点新花样了，到游戏结束一定很有趣。"劳拉不知道，"驾乘"才刚刚开始。

---

stride n. 大步；步幅   testy adj. 易怒的；暴躁的

Kelly backed off and rammed the fence again. Her trainer hurried to stop her. Using his training hook, he tried to turn Kelly away from the fence. But that just made the 8,000-pound animal madder. Kelly picked up her trainer with her trunk and *hurled* him across the ring like a *rag* doll. The children on Kelly's back kept screaming—but now their screams were from sheer terror.

The trainer got back on his feet. Again, he tried to control Kelly. But again, he failed. By this time, the elephant had broken through the fence. She charged toward the *bleachers*, where more than 2,000 people watched in shock. They knew that this wasn't part of the act. In panic, people *scrambled* over each other to reach the exits. An announcer's voice asked everyone to stay calm, but no one paid any attention to this request.

Then, suddenly, Kelly turned away from the bleachers. She

凯利向后退了退，又重重地撞在围栏上。它的训练员马上过来阻止它。他使用训练用的钩子试图把凯利从围栏拉开。但是这只能使这头8000磅重的大象更加狂躁。凯利用鼻子卷起了它的训练员，把他扔到了圈外，就好像是在扔一个布娃娃。在凯利后背上的孩子们开始尖叫起来——但是这次他们的尖叫完全是出于恐惧。

训练员站了起来，他再次试图控制凯利。但是他再次失败了。此时大象已经从围栏里面出来了。它冲向了露天看台，那里有2000名观众正在吃惊地观看着。他们知道这不是表演的一部分。人们十分惊恐，相互踩踏着向出口涌去。一个播音员的声音要求大家冷静，但是没有人听从这个要求。

突然，凯利从看台转向了别处。它开始用长鼻子撕扯架起帐篷的线

---

hurl *v.* 用力投掷   rag *n.* 破布
bleacher *n.* 露天看台   scramble *v.* 攀登；越过

reached up with her trunk and began to rip at the cables and wires that held up the tent. *Sparks* flew in all directions. A metal beam broke loose. It nearly hit Lawler and the five children, who were still on the elephant's back.

Meanwhile, another circus worker rushed to help. He climbed onto an elephant named Irene. He thought that if he could get Irene close to Kelly, he could grab the children out of the basket. As Irene moved in, Kathy Lawler picked up C. J.. She *leaned* out of the basket and handed her son to the man on Irene's back. Somehow, though, C. J. slipped out of the man's hands. The boy landed on the ground a few feet from Kelly's *stamping* feet.

"Get my kid!" yelled Lawler.

Luckily, someone rushed in and *dragged* C. J. to safety. Before Lawler could hand over any other children, though, Kelly knocked

---

缆，火花四散。一个金属架子松动了，差一点打中劳拉和五个孩子，他们现在还在大象的后背上。

另一名马戏团成员马上前来帮忙。他爬上了一头叫做艾琳的大象。他觉得如果他能够靠近凯利他就能够把孩子们从篮子里面接出来。当艾琳靠上来时，凯西·劳拉抓起了C. J.，她向前探出去，把她的孩子递给艾琳背上的人。但是不知怎么的，C. J. 从那个人的手中滑落了，男孩落到了离凯利踩踏的大脚只有几英尺的地方。

"抓住我的孩子！"劳拉大喊道。

幸运的是，有人冲了上来，把小C. J. 拖到了安全地点。在劳拉把第二个孩子递出去之前，凯利把艾琳撞到了一边。它冲出了帐篷，开始攻击

---

spark *n.* 火花　　　　　　　　　　lean *v.* 倾斜
stamp *v.* 用脚踩踏　　　　　　　　drag *v.* 拖拉

Irene out of the way. She went charging out of the tent and began to attack a car parked nearby. At that point, Police Officer Blayne Doyle came to the rescue. Doyle had been directing traffic outside the tent. He saw the elephant smash the car with her head and trunk. "She was very mad," Doyle said later.

Doyle ran up to the *crazed* beast. "Hand me one of the kids!" he shouted to Lawler.

But Kelly was too quick for him. She *whirled* her trunk around and knocked Doyle to the ground. Doyle scrambled to his feet. Once again he tried to get close to the elephant. This time Kelly grabbed him and pushed him face down in front of her.

Kathy Lawler watched in horror as the great *creature* tried to crush Doyle *beneath* her massive front legs. Doyle thought he had seen everything in his 22 years on the police force. But this was his

附近停着的一辆轿车。这时，警官巴列恩·多尔赶来营救。多尔在帐篷外面指挥交通。他看到了一头大象用它的头和鼻子打坏了一辆轿车。"它十分狂暴，"后来多尔这样说。

多尔冲向了发疯的大象。"给我一个孩子，"他向劳拉喊道。

但是凯利的动作很快。它转过了鼻子把多尔撞倒在地上，多尔爬了起来。他再次试图接近大象。这次凯利把他卷了起来，把他脸朝下摔在了前面。

凯西·劳拉恐怖地注视到这个巨大的动物想用脚把多尔压死。多尔认为他在警察局呆了22年，什么事情都见识过。但是这次是他最接近死亡的

crazed *adj.* 疯狂的　　　　　　　　whirl *v.* 使旋转
creature *n.* 动物；生物　　　　　　beneath *prep.* 在……之下

closest brush with death. He could barely breathe. He could feel Kelly crushing the life out of him. "In my lifetime," he later said, "I've been shot. I've been *stabbed*. I've *wrecked* police cars and police motorcycles. I've been in an airplane crash. But I've never been as scared as I was *underneath* that elephant."

Fortunately, a circus worker managed to distract Kelly by waving a training hook in front of her face. For a few seconds, she stopped her attack on Doyle. That was just long enough for someone else to *dart* in and pull Doyle away. Kelly, however, was still furious. She turned back to the car and banged at it some more. She didn't even notice the person who came close enough to reach up to the basket. Lawler handed down a child safely.

A moment later, Irene and her trainer came alongside again. Lawler managed to hand the three remaining children, one by one,

---

一次。他几乎不能呼吸，他能够感觉到凯利正在夺走他的生命。"在我一生中，"他后来说，"我被枪击中过，我被刺过。我的警车或者摩托车被撞毁过。我也曾遇到过飞机失事。但是我从来没有像被大象踩住时那么害怕。"

　　幸运的是，一名马戏团的工作人员尝试着用挥舞训练钩的方法把它的注意力吸引开。几秒钟之内，它停止了对多尔的攻击。这已经有足够时间让一个人冲进来，把多尔拉出来。但是凯利还是暴怒着，它转向了那个车子，继续向它发泄着，它甚至没有注意到有人靠近去动背上的篮子。劳拉安全地递下了一个孩子。

　　一会，艾琳和它的训练员再次来到了附近。劳拉尽力把3个剩余的孩子递过去，一个接着一个地，递给了训练员。然后劳拉自己跳到了艾琳的

---

stab *v.* 刺
underneath *prep.* 在……的下面

wreck *v.* 破坏；使失事
dart *v.* 猛冲

to the trainer. Then Lawler herself jumped onto Irene's back.

The drama was over for Kathy Lawler and the five frightened children. But it wasn't over for Kelly. Still as mad as ever, she moved on to attack a truck. She smashed in its side and ripped off a door. The truck's *jagged* metal cut the elephant's trunk, causing it to bleed.

Nothing could calm Kelly down. Her trainer knew what had to be done. "You're going to have to kill that elephant," he told Officer Doyle. "She's going to kill someone if you don't."

Doyle didn't want to shoot Kelly. "I love animals," he said later. He would have used a *tranquilizer* gun if he'd had one. That would have *knocked* Kelly *out* without killing her. But Doyle had only his regular gun. He hesitated a moment. But Kelly gave him no choice. She charged back toward the circus tent. There were still people inside.

背上。

对于凯西·劳拉和5个受到惊吓的孩子来说，这出戏结束了。但是凯利还是没有结束，它还是那么狂暴，开始攻击一辆卡车。它撞到了卡车的侧面，扯下了一个车门。卡车的钢板断面割坏了大象的鼻子，开始出血。

什么都无法使凯利安静下来。它的训练者知道该如何处置，"你必须得杀死那头大象，"他告诉多尔警官，"如果不开枪，它就会杀死人的。"

多尔不想射杀凯利。"我喜欢动物，"他后来说。如果他有镇静剂射枪他就会使用的。那可以使凯利晕过去，而不需要杀死它。但是多尔只有一支普通枪。他犹豫了一会。但是凯利不给他机会，它回过头，又冲向马

jagged *adj.* 锯齿状的
knock out 击昏；击倒

tranquilizer *n.* 镇静剂

Doyle knew he now had to shoot to kill.

Doyle ran beside Kelly, firing his pistol into the elephant's ear. Two other officers also opened fire. Wounded, but not slowed down, Kelly tore into the bleachers. The officers had to stop shooting. They did not want to hit anyone. They tried to direct people out of the tent. "Everyone was screaming and running," Doyle said. Then, with another sudden movement, Kelly turned and *bolted* out of the tent. Here, at last, an officer with a high-powered rifle killed her.

Doyle knew he had done his job. Still, he felt terrible. "I went over behind the wall and cried," he said. "We had to *destroy* one of God's most beautiful creatures."

戏团的帐篷，那里还有人，多尔知道现在他必须要开枪射杀它。

多尔跑到了凯利旁边，用手枪向大象的耳朵开枪，另外两名警察也开枪。凯利受了伤，但是没有停下来，它撕开了露天看台，警察们停止了开枪，他们不想伤到任何人，他们试图指挥人们跑出帐篷。"大家都在尖叫、逃跑，"多尔说。然后凯利又突然转过身，又逃出了帐篷。最后在这里，一名拿着强力步枪的警察把它打死了。

多尔知道他已经完成了他的工作。但是他还是感到很可怕，"我走到了墙脚，哭了，"他说，"我必须下手杀死一只上帝创造的最美的生物。"

---

bolt *v.* 逃跑　　　　　　　　　　　　　　destroy *v.* 破坏；毁灭

11

Tigers: Humans on the Menu

Quiz time: Which is more dangerous to humans—a healthy tiger or an injured tiger?

The answer is the injured tiger. Most healthy tigers want nothing to do with people. They're too busy chasing down deer and wild *hogs*. But what about a *disabled* tiger? *What if* it can no longer catch its natural prey? Imagine

The tiger is the largest member of the cat family. A healthy tiger normally feeds on large prey such as deer, antelope, and wild pigs. A sick or injured tiger may find it easier to attack slow-moving humans. Some tigers even develop a taste for humans.

猛虎伤人

老虎是猫科动物里面最大的。一只健康的虎以吃鹿、羚羊和野猪为生。有病或者受伤的虎发现攻击动作缓慢的人类更为容易。有些虎甚至出现了对人的偏爱。

小测试：对于人来说哪个更危险——健康的虎还是受伤的虎？

回答是受伤的虎。大部分健康的虎不喜欢和人打交道。它们忙于追逐鹿和野猪。但是一只受伤的虎呢？如果它已经无法捕杀它们天然的猎物怎

hog *n.* 猪
What if 要是……怎么办？

disabled *adj.* 伤残的

this tiger wandering through the fields. Think of its stomach *rumbling* with hunger. What do you guess it would do if it came upon a human being?

That was what happened in a remote part of Nepal in December 1979. There, a schoolteacher left his hut as he did every morning. He headed toward the river to wash up. This man wasn't the only one going to the river that day. A second man was walking about 50 yards behind the schoolteacher.

Meanwhile, a three-year-old tiger *padded* along the water's edge. The tiger walked slowly, with a deep *limp*. For the past year it had been unable to hunt its usual prey. A fight with another tiger had left it with a bad front leg. No longer could it *chase* down a fleet-footed deer. No longer could it take on a small elephant. It could not even

---

么办？想象一下这样的老虎在野地里面游逛。想象一下它的肚子空空，直打鼓。如果它遇到人它会怎么办？

那就是1979年12月，在遥远的尼泊尔的一个地区发生的一件事。那里一名学校教师像往常一样，在早晨离开了他的小屋，他到河边去洗漱。那天早晨他不是独自一个人去河边的，另一个人在他身后50码的地方走着。

当时，一只3岁大的虎在河岸上轻轻走着。老虎走得很慢，一瘸一拐。过去的一年里，它无法猎取天然的猎物。同其他一只虎的战斗使它的前腿受伤，它再也不能追赶跑得很快的鹿了，它也无法袭击小象了，甚至

---

rumble *v.* 隆隆作响
limp *n.* 跛行

pad *v.* 放轻脚步走
chase *v.* 追赶

manage to kill a wild pig.

To survive, the tiger had turned to farm animals. It had started to kill and eat cattle. It had also learned to eat the *buffaloes* that local farmers kept. Its new diet brought it closer and closer to the village, closer and closer to people.

That morning, the schoolteacher climbed the steep bank to the river. When he reached the top, he found himself face-to-face with the injured tiger. For a moment, neither one moved. Then the tiger *pounced* and the schoolteacher screamed. The man who had been 50 yards back hurried forward. He saw the schoolteacher trying to *ward off* the tiger. But it was no use. With a few *swipes* of its claws, the tiger ripped through the schoolteacher's clothes. The tiger's teeth tore into the teacher's body. Within seconds, the schoolteacher was

---

连一头野猪也无法杀死。

为了生存，这只虎转向了农场里面的牲畜。它开始猎取食用牛，它也学会了吃当地农民养的水牛。它的新食谱使它与村庄越来越近，与人越来越近。

那天早晨，学校教师爬上堤坝，来到了河边。当他走到了堤坝的顶端，发现他与一只受伤的老虎面对面。当时，双方都没有动。然后老虎跳了起来，教师尖叫了起来。后面50码远的人马上加快了速度赶了上来。他看到教师试图挡住老虎，但是没有用。老虎的爪子挥了几下，就撕开了教师的衣服。老虎的牙齿咬住了教师的身体。在几秒钟之内，教师就死了。

---

buffalo *n.* 水牛
ward off 避开；挡住

pounce *v.* 突袭；猛扑
swipe *n.* 猛击

dead.

The people in the village were shocked when they heard the news. Still, it was not the first time a tiger had attacked a person. In fact, tigers have killed thousands of people. From India to China to Vietnam, these beasts are known to be deadly to human beings.

Most man-eating tigers are old or disabled. Like the one that killed the schoolteacher, they can't catch wild prey. People in India saw this back in the 1930s. Villagers were *terrorized* by not one man-eating tiger, but 16. Slowly, these tigers were rounded up. All were found to have some kind of *injury*. Many had gunshot wounds. The rest had wounds caused by porcupine quills.

Sometimes, though, healthy tigers become man-eaters. This may happen when there is a shortage of wild prey in the region. Or

---

山村中的人们听到这个消息时震惊了。但是这也不是老虎第一次袭击人。实际上，老虎已经杀死了成千上万的人。从印度到中国到越南，这种动物是著名的人类杀手。

大部分吃人的老虎都是年老或者残疾。就像那只杀死了教师的老虎，他们无法捕杀野生猎物。早在20世纪30年代，印度的人们就见识了它们。村民不是被一只老虎吓住了，而是16只。这些老虎慢慢地集中到了一起。所有的都有点残疾。许多有枪伤。其他的有豪猪的刺伤。

有时，健康的虎也会吃人，当地的野生食物如果短缺，这种事情就

---

terrorize v. 使……恐怖

injury n. 受伤

it may happen *by accident*. If someone surprises a tiger, the animal may attack. Experts think that's what happened to Mahesh Howard. Howard was a grasscutter in India. One day in 1982 he went into the jungle. He must have come too close to a tiger's *den*. When Howard did not return, search parties went to look for him. They found his *bloodstained* clothes and six of his bones, *stripped* clean of flesh. In the mud next to these remains were the pawprints of a large tiger.

It was bad enough that Mahesh Howard had been killed and eaten. But his death was not the only sad part of the story. The tiger that killed him found that it liked the taste of human flesh. As one tiger expert says, "When an animal has killed and eaten a person, the danger is that it will add men to its menu."

And so it was in this case. In 1985 another grasscutter was in the

---

会出现。或者是偶然事件。如果有人使老虎受惊，它就会发动攻击。专家们认为这就是马赫什·豪伍德身上发生的事情。豪伍德是印度的一名割草人，在1982年的一天，他到丛林去，他一定是到了老虎巢穴很近的地方。豪伍德没有回来，搜索队伍出发去找他。他们找到了鲜血浸湿的衣服和他的6块骨头，上面已经没有肉了。在这些遗骸附近的泥巴里面有一只老虎的爪印。

马赫什·豪伍德一个人被老虎吃掉已经是够糟糕的事情了。但是他的死不是故事唯一的令人悲哀的部分。那只杀死他的老虎喜欢上了人肉的味道。正如一个老虎专家所说，"一旦动物捕杀并吃掉了人，危险在于它将人加入了它的菜单。"

---

by accident 偶然；意外地
bloodstained *adj.* 有血污的

den *n.* 兽穴
stripped *adj.* 削去的

same region. This man's name was Sudebar Ali. As Ali worked, he noticed a strange silence. There were no birds *chirping*, no monkeys *chattering*. Ali didn't know it, but he was being *stalked* by a tiger. Suddenly, the creature leaped out at him. Grabbing All's neck in its mouth, the tiger threw him into the air. Then it pounced on him, pinning him to the ground. The tiger bit through Ali's hand and *raked* its claws across his face. Luckily, a friend was nearby. The friend managed to distract the tiger while Ali escaped to safety. By the pawprints that the tiger left, game wardens knew that this tiger was the same one that had killed Mahesh Howard.

Tigers don't always have to kill people to acquire a taste for human flesh. In wartime, the bodies of dead soldiers may be left on the jungle floor. Tigers may start to feast on these bodies. That

---

所以这个事件发生了。1985年，另一名割草人来到了相同的地区，这个人叫作苏德巴·阿里。当阿里干活时，他注意到一种奇怪的寂静。没有鸟叫，没有猴子的私语。阿里不知道，一只老虎正在静静地跟随着他。突然，那个家伙向他扑去，它用嘴咬住了阿里的脖子，老虎把他抛到了空中。然后它又跳到了他的身上，把他按在地上。老虎咬穿了阿里的手，爪子划过了他的脸。幸运的是，一个朋友正在附近，这名朋友努力分散了老虎的注意力，阿里逃到了安全地带。从老虎留下的爪印来看，狩猎看护员知道这只老虎就是杀死马赫什·豪伍德的老虎。

老虎并不总需要杀人才能品尝到人肉。在战争时期，死亡士兵的尸体

---

chirp *v.* 唧唧叫

stalk *v.* 追踪

chatter *v.* 吱吱叫

rake *v.* 擦过

happened in World War II and again during the Vietnam War. In Vietnam, the tigers grew especially *bold*. They began to go after live soldiers. One tiger grabbed a U.S. marine right out of his foxhole. The man lived only because the tiger tried to drag him under a *barbed* wire fence. The marine got caught in the wire. That gave his fellow soldiers time to run over and drive the tiger off.

Researchers say there are other ways for tigers to learn to eat humans. One researcher thinks some may learn by watching their mothers. He says, "Females become man-eaters and teach their young to be man-eaters. [In time,] there is a whole crew of healthy man-eaters." Another researcher thinks salty water might be to blame. He believes high salt levels in drinking water may change a tiger's mood. That would explain why so many tigers in Bangladesh

---

被丢在丛林里面。老虎可能开始食用这些尸体。在二战时就发生了这样的事情，在越南战争中也发生了这样的事情。在越南老虎变得越来越大胆，他们开始跟随活着的士兵。一只老虎把一名美国海军陆战队员从散兵坑里面拖了出来。这个人活了下来是因为老虎试图拖着他穿过铁蒺藜网的下面，海军陆战队员抓住了铁蒺藜，这使其他士兵有足够的时间来冲上来，把老虎赶跑。

研究人员们说，还有其他的方法使老虎学会吃人肉。一些研究人员说，老虎可能通过观察它们的母亲学会的。他说："母老虎吃人，教会了小老虎吃人。这样，就会出现整群的吃人的老虎。"另外一些研究人员认为，应当责怪的是盐水。他认为老虎饮用的水中的高盐分子改变了老虎的

---

bold *adj.* 大胆的   barbed *adj.* 有刺的；有倒钩的

are man-eaters. There is not much fresh water there. The tigers must drink from the sea. Could that be why they are the most fearless and aggressive tigers in the world?

Humans may never *figure out* all the reasons why one tiger turns away and another pounces. One expert says that only a single tiger in 100 is a *hard-core* man-eater. That means only one in 100 will seek out human prey. But one in three will attack a human that crosses its path. Given this fact, many people fear tiger attacks will increase. After all, each year humans move deeper and deeper into the jungle. And as one Indian farmer says, it seems that "tigers and people cannot share space."

情绪。这就解释了为什么在孟加拉国有这么多的老虎吃人。那里的淡水少，老虎必须要喝海水。这就是它们成为世界上最无畏、最具有杀伤性的老虎的原因吗？

人们也许永远也解释不清为什么一只走开了，另一只又会跳上来。一名专家说100只老虎中只有一只是铁杆的吃人者。那就是说，在100只虎中只有一只在猎杀人，但是3个中有一个会攻击挡了它们路的人。根据这个事实，许多人害怕老虎的攻击会增加。毕竟，一年又一年，人们越来越深入地进入了丛林地带。正如一名印度农民所说的，看起来"老虎和人类无法分享空间。"

---

figure out　想出；理解　　　　　　　hard-core　*adj.* 最坚定的

12

Crocodiles:
The Jaws of Death

The crocodile *glided* through the water without a sound. Closer and closer it came. The young woman standing in the Daintree River did not *suspect* a thing. She was just cooling off during a picnic in the lovely Australian wilderness.

The crocodile stayed below the surface of the water as it approached.

It isn't hard to believe that this animal is dangerous, is it? The crocodile has many, many teeth, which it uses to grab its victims and pull them deep underwater.

死亡之鳄

不难相信这个动物很危险，是不是？鳄鱼有许多许多牙齿，用它们抓住受害者，并把它们拖入深水。

鳄鱼无声息地滑入了水中，它越来越近了。站在戴恩特利河里面的年轻女人没有怀疑任何事情。她刚刚在可爱的澳大利亚荒野中进行完野餐，想在河里凉快一下。

鳄鱼在接近时潜在水下。它平滑地，迅速地游动着。然后，突然爆

glide *v.* 滑行　　　　　　　　　　　　　　　　suspect *v.* 怀疑

It swam quickly, smoothly. Then, in one *explosive burst*, it opened its jaws and sank its teeth deep into the woman's flesh. The woman, whose name was Beryl Wruck, was never seen again. She another victim of Australia's deadly crocodiles. Since the late 1970s, these crocodiles have killed and eaten at least eight people.

Crocodiles look dangerous—and they are! At least three kinds are known to prey on human beings. First there is the saltwater crocodile, or "saltie". This was the kind that got Beryl Wruck. Found in Australia and parts of Asia, the saltie can grow to 28 feet. It may weigh more than 4,000 pounds. A second deadly crocodile is the *mugger*. It, too, lives in Asia. Finally, there is the Nile crocodile, which lives along the banks of the *mighty* Nile River in Africa.

Although salties are the biggest of the three, you would not want

---

发，张开了嘴，咬住了女人。这个女人的名字叫作伯伊尔·卢克，再也没有出现。她是澳大利亚吃人鳄鱼的又一个牺牲品。从20世纪70年代开始这些鳄鱼杀死并吃掉了8个人了。

鳄鱼看起来很危险——而且它们的确是的! 据所知，至少3种以人为食。首先有一种咸水鳄鱼，或者叫作"索提"。就是这种鳄鱼咬住了伯伊尔·卢克。它们生活在澳大利亚和亚洲的部分地区。索提能够长到28英尺。体重可以达到4000磅。第二种致命的鳄鱼是亚洲泽鳄，它也生活在亚洲。最后是尼罗河鳄鱼，它们生活在非洲巨大的尼罗河河岸上。

索提鳄鱼是3者中最大的，没人想同这3种鳄鱼打交道。它们都是凶

---

explosive adj. 爆发性的
mugger n. 泽鳄

burst n. 爆炸；爆发
mighty adj. 巨大的

to mess with any of these crocs. They are ferocious killers. If you *wander* into their *territory*, they won't think twice about eating you. To them, you're just another meal.

Crocodiles have been around since the time of the *dinosaurs*. They have lived in warm swamps and rivers for about 100 million years. During that time, they haven't changed much—they haven't needed to. They are among nature's most perfectly designed killing and eating machines.

A crocodile's body is long and flat, with rough, scaly skin. When it lies in the water, it looks like a floating log. But look again. You may see its nostrils and ears resting just above the water's surface. You may see two yellow eyes staring at you, waiting for you to come just a little closer. A crocodile's mouth is filled with about 70 razor-sharp

---

残的杀手。如果你进入了它们的领地，它们对于吃掉你的想法不会有一点点犹豫。对于它们来说，你就是一顿饭。

从恐龙的时代开始，鳄鱼就存在了。它们生活在温暖的沼泽和河流中已经有一百万年了。在此期间，它们并没有太大的变化——它们也完全没有必要改变。它们是自然创造的最为成功的捕杀和吃食的机器。

鳄鱼的身体长而且平，上面有粗糙的、带鳞片的皮肤。当它们在水中静静卧着时，看起来就好像是一块漂浮的木头。但是再仔细看看，你会发现它的鼻孔和耳朵刚刚露出水面。你可能也会看到一双黄色的眼睛正在打量着你，等待着你的距离再近一点。鳄鱼的嘴里布满了大约七十个像剃刀

---

wander *v.* 漫步；徘徊   territory *n.* 领土
dinosaur *n.* 恐龙

teeth. Its jaws are so strong that no creature on earth can pry them open once they have *clamped* shut.

With all those teeth, you might think a crocodile *chews* its victims to pieces. But it doesn't. In fact, crocodiles don't chew at all. A crocodile simply uses its teeth and jaws to grab onto its victim. Then it goes into a "death roll." Around and around it twirls, down through the water in a corkscrew spin. The idea is to *confuse* the prey. When at last the crocodile stops rolling, it holds its victim underwater. Usually the dazed victim drowns within a few minutes. But crocodiles don't mind if it takes longer. Crocs can hold their breath for up to one hour. Once the prey is dead, a crocodile pulls the dead body apart, swallowing the pieces in big *gulps*.

Hilton Graham is one of the lucky few to survive a crocodile

一样锋利的牙齿。它的下颚是如此的有力，以至于当它合上时，没有任何生物能够把它打开。

有这些牙齿，你可能会认为鳄鱼会把它的猎物嚼碎。但不是这样，实际上，鳄鱼根本就不咀嚼。鳄鱼使用它的牙齿仅仅是为了抓住它的猎物。然后它就进行"死亡旋转"。它一圈又一圈地进行旋转，在水里做螺旋状运动。目的是为了把猎物转晕。最后鳄鱼停止了转动，它把猎物拽下水。经常情况是转晕了的猎物在几分钟内就会被淹死。但是鳄鱼并不在意用的时间会长一些。鳄鱼可以屏住呼吸长达一个小时。当猎物死后，鳄鱼会把尸体撕开，然后大块地吞下去。

希尔顿·格拉海姆是在鳄鱼嘴下幸存的为数不多的人之一。1979年

---

clamp *v.* 夹紧；固定住
confuse *v.* 使困惑

chew *v.* 咀嚼
gulp *n.* 吞咽，一大口

attack. In 1979 Graham was boating in northern Australia. As he stepped *ashore*, a crocodile shot out of the water. Its jaws locked around Graham's waist. Thirteen-year-old Peta Lynn Mann saw what was happening. She grabbed Graham's hand and tried to pull him free.

The crocodile was too strong for Mann, however. It dragged both her and Graham into the water. Then, for some reason, the crocodile paused a moment. Perhaps it wanted to get a better grip on Graham's body. In any case, it *loosened* its hold just long enough for young Mann to pull Graham to safety. Although Graham lived, he was badly hurt. His arm was crushed. He had *internal* injuries. And his back was *riddled* with teethmarks the size of golf balls.

It isn't very often that a crocodile will open its jaws as one did

---

格拉海姆在澳大利亚的北部划船，正当他走上河岸时鳄鱼从水中冲了出来。它的大嘴咬住了格拉海姆的腰。13岁的派塔·林·曼看到了发生的事情，她抓住了格拉海姆的手，使劲想把他拉上来。

但是鳄鱼比曼要强壮。它把格拉海姆和她都拖进了水里。然后不知道为什么鳄鱼停止了一小会。可能是想更好的咬住格拉海姆的身体。但是它松动的时间已经足够使曼把格拉海姆拉到安全地带的了。虽然格拉海姆活了下来，但是他受了重伤。他的手臂骨折，也受了内伤。他的背上有许多高尔夫球大小的牙齿洞。

像攻击希尔顿·格拉海姆的鳄鱼那样松开嘴的鳄鱼并不多见。在攻击

---

ashore *adv.* 在岸上
internal *adj.* 内部的

loosen *v.* 放松；松开
riddle *v.* 将某人（某物）弄得满是窟窿

for Hilton Graham. Usually a crocodile is *relentless* in its attack. Crocodiles don't need to eat very often. They can go six months or more without food. Once they select a victim, though, they are *reluctant* to let it get away. Crocodiles have been known to jump several feet out of the water to get a meal. If necessary, they will even climb a tree to reach their prey.

Sandy Rossi knows how hard it is to get away from a hungry crocodile. In 1993 Rossi was serving as tutor and nanny to two American children in Zaire, Africa. On the afternoon of March 3, Rossi and the children were at the Epulu River. A friend was also there. As Rossi stood in the *muddy* water, a crocodile slid toward her. It grabbed her with such force that she was *knocked over*. She felt a sharp pain in her left arm. With a wave of horror, she realized she

---

当中，鳄鱼通常是无情的。鳄鱼不需要经常吃东西。它们可以一连6个月或者更长的时间不吃东西。一旦它们选择了猎物，它们很不愿意放掉。据我们所知，鳄鱼可以从水里跳出几英尺高来咬住猎物。如果需要的话，它们甚至可以爬到树上来接近猎物。

桑迪·罗西知道从饥饿的鳄鱼口中逃脱是多么的不容易。1993年，罗西在非洲的扎伊尔为两个美国孩子做家庭教师和保姆。在3月3日的下午，罗西和孩子们在艾普鲁河边玩，一个朋友也在那里。当罗西站在浑浊的河水中时，一条鳄鱼向她游去。它使了很大的力气咬住了罗西，以至于把罗西撞倒了。她感到她左胳膊上一阵剧烈的疼痛。在一阵恶浪里她知道

---

relentless *adj.* 无情的　　　　　　　　reluctant *adj.* 不情愿的
muddy *adj.* 泥泞的　　　　　　　　　　knock over 撞倒

was caught in the jaws of a crocodile.

Rossi managed to call out to her friend. Then she was dragged underwater. The death roll began. Over and over Rossi *tumbled* as the crocodile pulled her down. She felt the bones in her upper arm *snapping*. Her lungs burned, aching for fresh oxygen. When the death roll stopped, Rossi *summoned* all her strength. She pushed against the bottom of the river with her feet. She lifted herself up to the surface—with the crocodile still hanging onto her arm. She managed to breathe in some fresh air before the croc pulled her down and the death roll began again.

Several times the crocodile repeated its death roll. Each time, Rossi waited until the *spinning* stopped, then pushed up toward the surface. Meanwhile, her friend swam out to help her. Together the

是被鳄鱼咬住了。

罗西尽力呼喊她的朋友，然后她就被拖到了水下，死亡旋转开始了。罗西觉得鳄鱼在拖她下沉时一圈又一圈地旋转着。她感觉到上臂的骨头在折断，她的肺刺痛着，缺乏氧气。当死亡旋转停止时，罗西用尽全身的力气，尽力用脚推河床。她冒出了水面——鳄鱼垂在她的胳膊上。她尽力呼吸一些空气，可是鳄鱼又把她拖了下去，死亡旋转又开始了。

鳄鱼几次地重复着死亡旋转。每一次，罗西都等待着，直到死亡旋转停止，然后冲向水面。这时她的朋友游了过来帮助她。她们两个人一起与

tumble v. 滚动；摔倒
summon v. 鼓起；振作

snap v. 断裂并发出尖厉声音
spin v. 旋转

two of them wrestled the crocodile back toward shore. At last they managed to drag themselves out of the water. But when Rossi finally *wrenched* free of the crocodile, she left most of her arm behind. Her friend saw the crocodile open its jaws and swallow the *mass* of bone, muscle, and skin that it had been *grasping* between its teeth.

Survival stories like Sandy Rossi's and Hilton Graham's are rare. What happened to Ginger Faye Meadows is more typical. Meadows was an American who took a trip to western Australia. While there, she went for a swim along the Kimberly Coast. When she *dove* into the water, however, a crocodile was waiting for her. Meadows died in the saltie's huge jaws.

Clearly, you need to be very careful when you're in crocodile country. It's not enough to avoid the logs in the water. You must also be sure that the logs don't have ears, nostrils, and two yellow eyes.

鳄鱼较力，把它拉向河岸。最后她们终于露出了水面，但是当罗西最终从鳄鱼的嘴里挣脱出来时，她把她手臂的大部分留在了里面。她的朋友看到鳄鱼张开了嘴，把牙齿间咬住的骨头、肉和皮肤一股脑地吞了下去。

向桑迪·罗西和希尔顿·格拉海姆这样的幸存故事太少见了。在金吉尔·法耶·米都斯身上发生的事情更为典型。米都斯是一位到澳大利亚西部旅行的美国人。在那里她到金伯里海滩去游泳。当她潜入水中时，正赶上一条鳄鱼在等着她。米都斯死在索提鳄鱼的巨口之中。

很明显，在鳄鱼出没的地方你要十分小心。仅仅避开水中的木头还不够，你必须弄清楚，这些木头没有耳朵、鼻孔和两个黄色的眼睛。

---

wrench *v.* 猛扭   mass *n.* 块

grasp *v.* 抓住；控制   dive *v.* 潜水；跳水

13

Killer Bees

Christopher Graves didn't have time to run away. One moment he was starting up his *lawn mower* and the next moment he was completely covered with angry, stinging bees. The attack came on August 23, 1994. Graves was at his grandmother's home in Texas. He had planned to cut the grass for her. But

Running into killer bees would ruin any outdoor activity. They gang up on their victims, attacking by the thousands.

杀人蜂

遇到杀人蜂就会毁掉任何室外的活动的计划。它们不是一次一只的进行攻击，而是成千上万地成群攻击受害者。

克里斯托佛·格拉夫斯根本没有时间逃跑。刚才还在发动一个草坪割草机，现在就被愤怒的蜇人蜜蜂覆盖了全身。这次攻击发生在1994年8月23日，格拉夫斯在得克萨斯他祖母的家里面。他计划为她修理草坪，但是

lawn *n.* 草坪　　　　　　　　　　　　mower *n.* 割草机

when the 20-year-old Graves started the mower, he upset a swarm of bees in the area.

Graves saw the first bee come at him. He felt its sting.

"In the next blink of my eye," he said, "I was just covered."

Indeed, about 4,000 bees had appeared out of nowhere. They *buzzed* furiously around Graves. They stung him more than 1,000 times. Each sting carried just a small amount of poison. But all together, the stings threatened his life. *By the time* firefighters arrived and got him to the hospital, Graves was in serious condition.

This was not the first time bees had attacked a human, and it would not be the last. In fact, since 1957, more than 1,000 people have been killed in bee attacks. Countless more have fought off angry bees and survived.

One survivor was 51-year-old Leonard Salcido. On August 16,

当20岁的格拉夫斯发动了割草机时，他惊动了这个地区的一群蜜蜂。

格拉夫斯看到第一个蜜蜂向他冲来，他感到被叮了一下。

"我的眼睛刚刚一眨，我的身上就落满了，"他说。

实际上，大约四千只蜜蜂不知从哪里冒了出来。它们围绕着格拉夫斯疯狂地嗡嗡叫着，它们叮了他一千多次，每一次只是一点点毒素。但是这么多毒素实际上影响到了他的生命。当消防队员们赶到，把他送到医院的时候，格拉夫斯已经处于危险中了。

这不是蜜蜂第一次袭击人类，这也不会是最后一次。实际上，从1957年开始，大约一千多人在这样的袭击中死亡。也有无数的其他人击败了愤怒的蜜蜂而生存了下来。

一个幸存者是51岁的列奥纳多·萨尔西多。在1997年8月16日，他在

---

buzz *v.* 嗡嗡叫　　　　　　　　　　　　　by the time 到……时候

1997, he was mowing his backyard in New Mexico. Salcido knew there was a *beehive* in the fence at the edge of the lawn. But he wasn't worried about it. It had been there for a long time. In the winter, he and his family gathered honey from it. The noise of the lawn mower never seemed to bother the bees at all.

But on this day, the bees went crazy.

"It was like a horror movie," said Salcido's daughter. "My dad was mowing the yard when we looked out and saw him running toward the water *hose*. I ran out of the house and *grabbed* the hose and tried to *spray* him down with water. The bees came for me. They were everywhere. The water was not getting them off my dad." By the time Salcido got away from the bees, he had been stung over 100 times.

Stories like Graves's and Salcido's are becoming more and more

---

新墨西哥州的家中修建草坪。萨尔西多知道在草坪的边缘篱笆里面有一个蜂巢，但是他没有担心。它已经在那里好长时间了。在冬季，他和家人从里面取出了蜂蜜。割草机的噪音好像从来就没有影响过那里的蜜蜂。

但是在今天，蜜蜂们发起疯来。

"就好像是恐怖电影，"萨尔西多的女儿说，"我的父亲正在修剪草坪，突然我们向外看时，他冲向了水管。我冲出了房间，尽量给他全身浇水。蜜蜂们开始来袭击我，它们到处都是，水也没有把它们赶走。"当萨尔西多从蜜蜂的包围下逃出来时，他已经被叮了一百多次。

像格拉夫斯和萨尔西多这样的故事变得越来越平常。这是因为在美国

---

beehive *n.* 蜂巢
grab *v.* 攫取；抓住

hose *n.* 软管
spray *v.* 喷射

common. That's because there is a new kind of bee in America. Scientists refer to it as the "Africanized bee". But most people just call it the killer bee.

Long ago there were no honeybees of any kind in North or South America. Then, in the 1600s, Europeans brought some over. These European bees quickly *adapted* to life in North America. They set up colonies. They built hives and produced honey. But down in Latin America, these bees did not do so well. They didn't care for the hot, humid climate. As a result, little honey was produced in Latin America. If folks there wanted honey, they had to ship it in from the north.

In the 1950s, scientists hoped to change that situation. They wanted to *breed* honeybees that liked hot weather. They knew that African bees did well in hot climates. But African bees were much

---

有一种新的蜜蜂，科学家称之为"非洲化的蜜蜂"。但是大多数人就管它叫作杀手蜜蜂。

很久以前，在北美和南美没有任何种类的蜜蜂。在17世纪，欧洲人带来了一些，这些欧洲的蜜蜂很快就适应了北美的生活。它们开始建立蜂巢，开始酿蜜。但是在拉丁美洲，这些蜜蜂的工作却不太好。它们不是很适应当地炎热潮湿的气候，结果是在拉丁美洲几乎没有产出什么蜂蜜。如果人们需要蜂蜜就需要从北方运来。

在20世纪50年代，科学家希望能够改变这个情况。他们希望能够培育出喜欢炎热天气的蜜蜂。他们知道非洲的蜜蜂在炎热气候中做得很好。但是非洲的蜜蜂比欧洲的蜜蜂更具有进攻性，它们更容易受惊，而且如果

---

adapt *v.* 适应   breed *v.* 繁殖；饲养

more aggressive than the European *variety*. They were more easily disturbed. And when they got angry, they attacked in large numbers.

Still, scientists thought the African bees could be helpful. They brought some to a laboratory in Brazil. They never meant to *release* the bees into the open. Instead, they planned to keep them locked away in the lab. There they could *crossbreed* them with European bees. In time, they hoped to get a new and improved bee. It would have the gentle personality of European bees. But it would have the African bees' love of hot weather.

It sounded like a good plan. But something went wrong. In 1957, a group of African bees escaped from the lab. They flew out into the wild. Soon they began to take over local *hives*. The result was not what scientists had been hoping for. The new bees certainly liked hot weather. But their personalities were far from mellow. One scientist

---

它们发怒，它们将大量地进行袭击。

但是，科学家们认为非洲蜜蜂会有帮助。他们把一些非洲蜜蜂送到了巴西的实验室。他们从来没有打算把它们放到自然中，实际上他们决定将它们关在实验室里面。在那里他们可以进行非洲蜜蜂和欧洲蜜蜂的杂交。他们希望这样能够获得一种改良品种。它应该有一些欧洲蜜蜂的个性。也具有非洲蜜蜂对于炎热天气的偏爱。

听起来是个不错的计划。但是出现了问题。1957年，一群非洲蜜蜂从实验室逃了出来，它们逃到了外面的世界里。很快它们开始在当地落户。结果并不是科学家们所希望的那样。新的蜜蜂当然喜欢炎热的天气，但是它们的性格可一点也不温和。一个科学家称它们是"有性格的蜜蜂"。

---

variety *n.* 品种　　　　　　　　　　　release *v.* 释放
crossbreed *v.* 杂交　　　　　　　　　hive *n.* 蜂巢

called them "honeybees with an attitude."

"All honeybees have bad days," the scientist explained. But for the new Africanized bees, every day is a bad day. These bees are 10 times as aggressive as European bees. It takes European bees about 19 seconds to get *irritated* enough to sting. It takes Africanized bees just 3 seconds.

And that's not all. European bees will chase a person for only about 400 meters. Africanized bees will follow their targets for a *metric* mile.

Africanized bees work in large groups. So people are rarely stung by just one or two. If these bees feel *threatened*, they send huge numbers rushing out to attack.

Could the news get any worse? Yes. Consider this: it takes just one Africanized bee to *drastically* change a whole colony of European

---

"所有的蜜蜂都有不舒服的日子，"科学家解释道。但是对于这些新的非洲化的蜜蜂，每一天都不舒服，它们比欧洲蜜蜂的攻击性强10倍。欧洲蜜蜂要用19秒的时间才能被激怒到叮人状态。但是非洲化的蜜蜂只需要3秒钟。

而这又不是全部的问题。欧洲蜜蜂会追赶400米。非洲化的蜜蜂将追出1000米。

非洲化的蜜蜂在大群里面生存，所以人们很少被一两只叮咬。如果这些蜜蜂觉得受到了威胁，它们将派大量的蜂群进行攻击。

这个新闻带来更糟糕的消息吗？是的。考虑一下这个情况：仅仅一只非洲化的蜜蜂就极大地改变了欧洲蜜蜂的整个种群。专家认为这就是在里

---

irritated *adj.* 恼怒的
threatened *adj.* 受到威胁的

metric *adj.* 公制的；米制的
drastically *adv.* 彻底地

bees. Experts think that's what happened in Leonard Salcido's case. One killer bee might have found its way into his peaceful backyard hive. In just 45 days, that one bee could have *transformed* the colony. Instead of European bees, the hive would have been filled with Africanized bees.

Experts point out that killer bees attack only when they feel threatened. So the key is to stay far away from them. That advice would have helped Chisha Chang. On August 3, 1998, the 88-year-old Chang found a beehive attached to his *barbecue grill*. He thought he could remove it himself. So he put a plastic bag over his head for protection. Then he reached down to pull out the hive.

Suddenly, dozens and dozens of bees flew out at Chang. They *swarmed* all over him. Many got up inside the plastic bag. They stung him all over his face and head.

昂那多·萨尔西多事件中发生的事情。一只杀手蜜蜂可能进入了他后院的蜂巢，仅仅过了45天，这一只蜜蜂就改变了整个蜂巢。现在这个蜂巢里面已经不是欧洲蜜蜂了，里面将充满非洲化的蜜蜂。

专家指出，杀手蜜蜂只有当它们觉得受到了威胁才会发动攻击，所以关键是远离它们。这个建议可能帮助了奇沙·常。在1998年8月3日，88岁的常发现他的烤肉架上面有一个蜂巢。他想他应该自己把它摘掉，所以他用一个塑料袋子套在头上作为保护，然后他探了下去把蜂巢扯了下去。

突然，一群又一群的蜜蜂飞向了常，它们裹住了他的全身。许多进入了塑料袋子，它们在他的脸上和头上开始叮。

---

transform *v.* 改变
grill *n.* 烤架

barbecue *n.* 烤肉
swarm *v.* 成群飞行

Police and firefighters were called to the scene. Said one firefighter, "I would describe him as having a hive of bees on his face. You could not see his eyes or his nose. It was like a hive being taken out of a tree and placed on his head."

A rescue worker managed to pull the bag off Chang's face and move him to safety. Luckily, Chang survived the attack. Later, a specially trained beekeeper removed the hive from the grill. He *estimated* that it contained 70,000 bees.

Today, killer bees are a fact of life in Texas, New Mexico, Arizona, and California. But the rest of the United States doesn't have much to worry about. Africanized bees still love hot weather. Whenever they *stray* to colder regions, they die. And that's good news for anyone who likes to mow the lawn in peace.

　　警察和消防队员被叫到了事发现场。一名消防队员说："我应该说他的脸上简直就成了蜂巢。你看不到他的眼睛和鼻子。就好像是一个蜂巢从树上摘了下来，放到了他的头上。"

　　一名营救人员把塑料袋子从他的头上拉了下来，把他送到了一个安全地带。幸运的是常在这次袭击中幸存了下来。后来一名受过专门训练的养蜂人取下了烤肉架上面的蜂巢。他估计里面有70,000只蜜蜂。

　　今天，杀手蜜蜂成为得克萨斯、新墨西哥、亚里桑那和加利福尼亚的生活中的一部分。但是美国的其他部分没有太多需要担心的。非洲化的蜜蜂还是太喜欢炎热的气候，它们只要一到寒冷地区，就会死亡。这对于那些喜欢在平静中修建草坪的人来说无疑是个好消息。

---

estimate v. 估计

stray v. 偏离；走失

14

Cougars on the Prowl

Iris Kenna liked to watch rare birds. To find them, the 56-year-old school *counselor* often hiked in the Cuyamaca Rancho State Park near San Diego. But in 1995 Kenna found something she wasn't looking for—a *cougar*. Caught by surprise, Kenna never had a chance. The wild cat dragged her off the path and

Cougars were once quite common throughout the United States and southern Canada. As settlers moved in and populated these areas the cougars' numbers dropped. Today, cougars are found mainly in western U.S. and Canadian provinces.

觅食的美洲狮

在整个美国和加拿大的南部，美洲狮曾经一度十分常见。随着定居者的迁入并在这些地区繁衍生息，美洲狮的数目下降了。今天，主要在美国西部各州和加拿大的一些省中可以找到美洲狮。

艾力斯·肯娜喜欢看稀有鸟类。为了找到它们，这位56岁的学校顾问经常在圣迭戈附近的库雅马卡·兰奇奥州立公园里面登山。但是1995年，肯娜发现了一个她不想寻找的东西——美洲狮。肯娜惊呆了，她根本没有机会。这头狮子把她拖到路边的树丛中，它用尖利的爪子和牙齿要了

counselor *n.* 顾问　　　　　　　　　　　　cougar *n.* 美洲狮

into some *dense* brush. With its sharp claws and piercing teeth, the cougar soon claimed Kenna's life. At some point in the struggle, it ripped off part of her *scalp*. Park *rangers* later found Kenna's dead body covered with bite marks.

Laura Smalls was only five years old when she was attacked by a cougar. In 1986 she went exploring with her parents in California's Gaspers Wilderness Park. For a few seconds, she wandered off by herself. That was a mistake. A cougar leapt at her and pulled her into the bushes. "All I heard was a *rustle* in the bushes behind me," Laura recalled. "A split second later [the cougar] had me by the head."

Luckily, Laura's screams brought her parents running. They managed to beat off the cougar with a stick. That probably saved the girl's life. Still, the attack left her blind in her right eye. It also left

---

肯娜的命。在挣扎过程中，狮子撕掉了肯娜的一块头皮。后来公园管理员发现了肯娜的尸体，上面有许多咬过的痕迹。

当劳拉·斯莫尔思遭到美洲狮袭击时仅仅5岁。1986年她和父母到加利福尼亚的卡斯普尔斯荒野公园探险。她自己单独行动了仅仅几秒钟的时间，这是一个错误。一头美洲狮扑向了她，把她拖进了树丛中。"我只是听到身后的树丛中一阵沙沙声，"劳拉回忆道，"一眨眼的工夫，[美洲狮]就叼住了我的头。"

幸运的是，劳拉的尖叫声使她的父母跑了过来，他们尽了全力用棒子打跑了美洲狮。可能是这个行动拯救了女孩的生命。但是这次被美洲狮袭击使她的右眼失明，也使她部分残疾。

---

dense *adj.* 稠密的　　　　　　　　　　　　scalp *n.* 头皮
ranger *n.* 管理员　　　　　　　　　　　　rustle *n.* 沙沙声

her partially *paralyzed*.

Cougars go by many names. They are called mountain lions, catamounts, panthers, and pumas. Whatever name you prefer, keep in mind that these are dangerous creatures. They are fierce meat eaters. They hunt deer, *elk*, rabbits, and other animals. Cougars are patient in their *quest* for food. A cougar will *stalk* its prey until just the right moment. Then it will lunge at the victim's throat or neck. Given a choice, a cougar will choose the weakest prey and attack from behind.

Cougars don't often attack human beings. But when they do, they usually go for women or children. Men, who tend to be bigger and taller, may simply look too tough for a cougar to take on.

Cougar attacks have increased in recent years. This is especially

---

美洲狮有许多名字。它们被称为山狮、野猫、山猫、黑豹、美洲狮等等。无论你使用什么名字，要记住，它们都是危险的动物，它们是凶猛的食肉动物。它们捕杀鹿、麋鹿、兔子和其他动物。美洲狮对捕食很有耐性。美洲狮在时机到来之前会一直静静地跟踪猎物。然后它会突然扑上去咬住受害者的喉咙或者脖子。如果有机会，美洲狮会选择最弱小的猎物，并且从身后攻击。

美洲狮通常不袭击人。但是它们如果攻击人的话，经常攻击妇女和儿童，男人的体形高大，看起来美洲狮对付不了。

在近些年来，美洲狮的袭击有所增长，尤其在西部各州更是这样。每

---

paralyzed *adj.* 瘫痪的
quest *n.* 追求；寻找

elk *n.* 麋鹿
stalk *v.* 追踪

true in western states. Each year, more people move there. New homes are being built closer and closer to where cougars live. So bloody *encounters* are likely to become more *frequent*.

What would happen if you found yourself eyeball-to-eyeball with a cougar? Would you have any chance of surviving the attack? Actually, you'd have a good chance—if you knew what to do. The first rule is never run away. That's what a cougar's other victims do. You don't want to act like a deer or a rabbit. If you do, the cougar will quickly run you down and *finish you off*.

Your best *strategy* is to look as big as possible. Stand tall, with your arms raised. Then slowly back away. If the cougar still attacks, stay on your feet and fight back! A cougar is used to attacking helpless prey. It may become confused, even frightened, if you

---

一年，越来越多的人移居到那里。人们的新家与美洲狮距离越来越近，所以血腥的对抗就经常发生了。

如果你发现你自己正好和一只美洲狮直面相对，会发生什么事情？你能否从它的袭击中幸存下来呢？实际上，你有很好的机会——如果你知道该如何去做。法则一是不要逃跑。那是其他美洲狮的受害者的所作所为。你不要表现出像个鹿或者兔子的样子。如果你那样做，美洲狮会迅速地追上你，要了你的命。

你最好的战略是看起来尽可能地高大。要站直，上臂举起。然后缓慢地后退。如果美洲狮还是发动了攻击，你要站稳然后回击！美洲狮经常袭击无助的猎物。如果你与它打斗它可能会被迷惑甚至害怕。你要刺向它的

---

encounter *n.* 遭遇
finish sb off 毁坏某人

frequent *adj.* 频繁的
strategy *n.* 策略；战略

put up a fight. Poke it in the eyes, *kick* it in the groin, *punch* it in the mouth. Pick up a heavy stick and imagine you are taking batting practice—with the cougar's head as the baseball. Most cougars will flee when faced with *stiff* resistance.

For a dramatic example, take the case of Larrane Leech. She ran a day-care center out of her home in British Columbia. Leech loved the outdoors. She wanted the children to enjoy it, too. And they did. Their favorite activity was circle time. The kids would sit outdoors in a circle and pass around an eagle feather. Whoever held it could talk about anything he or she wanted.

On July 3, 1991, Leech took five children for a walk to the Fraser River. Her German *shepherd* puppy, Pal, went with them. The children picked berries along the way. Finally, Leech called to them to "get in

---

眼睛，踢它的腰，用拳头打它的嘴，可以拾起一根大棒，想象你在进行击球练习——把美洲狮的脑袋想象成为垒球。当遇到强硬的反抗时大部分的美洲狮会逃跑。

有一个很戏剧化的例子，比如拉伦·里奇。她在英属哥伦比亚地区开了一家白天托儿所。里奇喜欢户外活动，她也希望孩子们喜欢。而且他们的确也很喜欢。他们最喜欢的活动是围成圈的时候，它们在户外坐成一圈，传递一支鹰的羽毛。任何一个拿着羽毛的人要说出他/她想要什么。

在1991年的7月3日，里奇带着5个孩子在法拉塞河边散步。她的一只叫作帕尔的德国牧羊犬幼犬跟着她。孩子们在路上采着草莓。最后里奇让

---

kick *v.* 踢

stiff *adj.* 坚硬的

punch *v.* 用拳猛击

shepherd *n.* 牧羊犬

our circle." One little girl, however, ran off toward some trees. Leech hurried to *retrieve* her.

As Leech headed back to the circle with the girl, her face froze in terror. A young cougar had appeared from the bushes. It had a two-year-old boy named Mikey pinned to the ground. From where Leech stood, she couldn't see Mikey's face. She couldn't tell if he was alive or dead. None of the other children seemed to understand what was happening. To them, the cougar looked like an *overgrown* house cat. "Stop licking Mikey's face," one of them *giggled*.

Leech didn't stop to think about her own safety. Her only thought was to rescue Mikey. She charged toward the cougar, intending to grab its tail. At the last second, though, she grabbed it by the *scruff* of its neck. She shook the cougar from side to side. "I couldn't tell if

他们"进到圈子里面"。但是一个小女孩向外围的树林跑去，里奇急忙过去把她找回来。

当里奇领着小女孩向圈子走回去时，她的脸上被恐惧凝住了。一只小美洲狮从树丛中钻了出来，它把一个两岁大的叫作米奇的男孩按倒在地上。从里奇站着的地方无法看到男孩的脸，她也无法看出他是活着还是死了。其他的孩子们都不知道发生了什么事情。对于他们来说，美洲狮看起来就好像是一只长得很大的家猫。"别舔米奇的脸，"一个孩子傻里傻气地哈哈笑着说。

里奇没有停下来考虑她自己的安危。她唯一的念头是营救米奇，她向美洲狮冲了过去，想抓住它的尾巴。但是最后，她抓住了它的后颈。她使劲地摇晃着美洲狮。"我不知道它是不是咬住了米奇的脸，还是它打算把

retrieve *v.* 重新得到
giggle *v.* 咯咯地笑

overgrown *adj.* 生长过快的
scruff *n.* 后颈

he had Mikey's face in his mouth, or if he would rip him apart," she later recalled. "So I just shook him."

As it turned out, the cougar had not yet bitten Mikey. It was a young cougar; it had not learned to make a fast, efficient attack. Instead, it was licking the boy's face clean in preparation for its first bite. When Leech grabbed its neck, it shifted into a more *vicious* attack mode. It whirled toward her, *hissing* and spitting. As it spun, its claws caught Mikey in the face. These claws also *nicked* Lisa, not quite two years old, under her eye. Leech fell backward as the cougar's powerful paw *smacked* her across her right ear.

The children now realized that this was no game. They began screaming in terror. They raced to hide behind Leech. "Stay behind me!" she shouted to them. "Don't move."

他撕成几块，"后来她回忆道，"所以我就是使劲地摇晃着。"

但是，后来发现美洲狮还没有开始咬米奇。它只是一只小狮子；还没有学会如何进行迅速有效的攻击。实际上，它正在把米奇的脸舔干净，作好准备咬第一口。当里奇抓住它的脖子时，它就摆出了一副更凶恶的攻击姿态。它转过身子，发出嘶嘶声，喷着唾沫。当它转过身的时候，它的爪子抓了米奇的脸。这个爪子也在丽莎的脸上留下了痕迹，丽莎还不到两岁，划在了眼睛下面。美洲狮有力的爪子打在里奇的右耳上，把她打倒在地上。

这时孩子们意识到这不是游戏。他们开始恐惧地尖叫起来。他们冲到里奇的身后。"躲在我的后面！"她向他们喊道，"别动。"

---

vicious *adj.* 恶意的

nick *v.* 在……上划刻痕

hiss *v.* 发出嘘声

smack *v.* 用掌击

Leech managed to grab the cougar's front paws. She *straightened* out her arms, holding the animal as far away from her body as she could. The cougar *growled* angrily and tried to pull free from her grip. Her arms and legs ached as the cat thrashed furiously back and forth. Yet Leech held on, knowing that if the cougar broke away from her it could kill the children. "Leave us alone," she screamed at the cat, "and we'll leave you alone!"

Calling on all her remaining strength, Leech *shoved* the cougar at her German shepherd. "Pal, do something!" she cried. As Pal began to bark, the cougar scrambled to its feet. Then it dashed away, with Pal still barking after it.

Larrane Leech had done the right thing. By putting up a fight and *yelling* in a loud voice, she had scared the cougar. Amazingly, she

---

里奇尽力抓住美洲狮的前爪。她伸直了手臂，尽量把它支得远些。美洲狮愤怒地咆哮着想从她的手中挣脱。随着美洲狮的前后挣扎，里奇的手臂和腿又酸又疼。但是里奇竭尽全力抓住它，她知道如果它挣脱了，就可能伤到孩子们。"离我们远些，"她对着美洲狮尖叫着，"我们也不会去碰你！"

里奇使出了她全身的力气，把狮子扔向德国牧羊犬。"帕尔，干活！"她大喊着。帕尔开始吠叫，美洲狮挣扎着站了起来，飞快地逃跑了，帕尔追在后面吠叫着。

劳林·里奇的行动完全是正确的。她通过打斗和高声喊叫把美洲狮吓

---

straighten v. （使某物）变直　　　growl v. 咆哮
shove v. 挤；猛推　　　yell v. 大叫；叫喊

suffered only minor cuts and *scratches*. Mikey needed 40 *stitches*. Little Lisa needed 20. All the children were very fortunate. If Leech had not acted as she did, the incident could have ended in tragedy.

The Canadian government knows a hero when it sees one. It awarded Larrane Leech its Star of Courage for "outstanding bravery." Leech *modestly* noted that "any parent would have done the same." Perhaps. But how many parents have ever gone face-to-face with a wild cougar?

着了。令人惊奇的是，她仅仅是受了划伤这样的小伤。米奇缝了40针，小丽莎缝了20针。所有的孩子们都很幸运。如果里奇不是那样反应，这个事故就可能是以悲剧结局。

加拿大政府是不会埋没一个英雄的。它授予劳林·里奇一枚"勇敢之星"，以表彰她"突出的勇气"。里奇谦虚地说："任何家长都会这样做的。"也许吧，但是有多少家长能与一只野生的美洲狮面对面呢？

---

scratch *n.* 擦伤   stitch *n.* 一针
modestly *adv.* 谦虚地

15

Scorpions: Killers in the Desert

Ross Brown ran up to his mother, holding his finger and crying. At first, Karen Brown guessed that he had been bitten or stung by some sort of insect. But when she looked closely, she couldn't see any *mark* on the boy's finger. Karen *figured* Ross, who was only one week shy of his first birthday, was simply overtired.

This scorpion mom carries her newborn brood on her back. These babies are lucky. Because their mother is in an exhibit and will be fed, they don't have to worry about her forgetting family ties and eating them.

沙漠杀手

这只蝎子妈妈在背上背着新生下来的一窝小蝎子。这些小蝎子很幸运，因为它们的妈妈正在展览而且会得到食物，它们不用担心妈妈忘记了血缘关系而吃掉它们。

罗斯·布朗向他的母亲跑去，抓住指头，哭了起来。开始，凯伦猜想到他是被什么昆虫咬到或者叮到了。但是当她贴近了仔细看时，她没有发现男孩的手指上有任何的痕迹。罗斯还有一周就到一岁的生日了，凯伦认

mark *n.* 痕迹

figure *v.* 认为

But soon the boy's crying turned to screaming. He began to *vomit* and shake violently all over. That was when Karen knew something was seriously wrong with her son.

It was May 1994. Karen and her husband, Don, had been packing the family car when Ross began crying. The Browns were about to head home after a trip to Mexico. They had loved their weekend stay in the desert along the Gulf of California. But suddenly they were in a life-or-death race to save their son.

At first, the Browns looked for a local hospital. When they could not find one, they decided to head back to Arizona. As the Browns sped north to the border, Ross grew *steadily* worse. His eyes rolled back and forth in his head. His nose and mouth foamed. He had trouble breathing. His skin turned pale, and his heart raced furiously.

The Browns had no way of knowing it at the time, but Ross had

---

为他可能是太累了。但是很快孩子的哭声变成了尖叫声，他开始呕吐并且全身剧烈地发抖。这时凯伦才意识到她的儿子出现了严重的问题。

那是1994年的5月，凯伦和她的丈夫，唐正在给家用轿车打包，突然罗斯开始哭泣。布朗一家在墨西哥结束旅行后正打算回家。他们很喜欢在加利福尼亚海湾边上的沙漠中度过周末。但是突然他们要展开生死时速来拯救他们的儿子。

刚开始，布朗一家开始找当地的医院，但是无法找到。他们决定回头前往亚里桑那。当布朗一家冲向北部的边境时，罗斯的状况变得更糟糕了。他的眼睛上下翻动，鼻子和嘴出现白沫，他的呼吸出现困难，他的皮肤变得苍白，而心脏跳动的速度加快。

当时，布朗一家根本不知道，罗斯被蝎子蜇到了。很久以前在现在墨

---

vomit *v.* 呕吐　　　　　　　steadily *adv.* 持续地；不断地

been stung by a scorpion. Long ago, the Maya people, who lived in an area located in what today is Mexico and Central America, had a word for the scorpion. It meant "sign of the death god". There are about 1,500 types of scorpions in the world. They all have poisonous *venom*. But only about 25 kinds have venom strong enough to kill a human being. Most of these scorpions are found in India, Brazil, and North Africa. In such places, thousands of people die each year from scorpion stings.

One of the *lethal* scorpions is also found in the deserts of Mexico and Arizona. It is the *bark* scorpion. It got this name because it often lives under the loose bark of dead trees. The sting of a bark scorpion leaves no *visible* mark on its victim.

All scorpions are night creatures. They wait until dark to come out

---

西哥和中美洲地区居住的玛雅人有一个词语来形容蝎子，叫作"死神的标志"。在世界上有1500种蝎子，它们都有毒，但是其中只有25种的毒液足以杀死人。这些蝎子的大部分存在于印度、巴西和北美。这些地区，每年成千上万的人死于蝎子的叮咬。

其中一种致命的蝎子可以在墨西哥和亚里桑那州的沙漠中找到。它们被称为树皮蝎子，因为它们经常生活在死树的树皮下面。树皮蝎子叮过的地方是一点痕迹都没有的。

所有的蝎子都是夜间行动的动物。它们等黑暗时才出来觅食，有时它

---

venom *n.* 毒液
bark *n.* 树皮

lethal *adj.* 致命的
visible *adj.* 看得见的

of hiding and eat. Sometimes they fight each other, with the winner eating the loser. Other times they use their *venomous* tails to kill beetles, *wasps*, spiders, and crickets.

Scorpions do not wander far away to hunt. Often they travel only a few feet from their home. They identify a spot they like and then settle down for the night, waiting for something to kill. If nothing comes along before sunrise, they'll go home. Scorpions see poorly, but they are good hunters nonetheless. They use their body hair to detect changes in the movement of the air. That's how they sense the presence of prey. If something does come along, the scorpion will seize it with its two *pincers*.

All scorpions are *mean*. They don't like anyone—not even each other. If hungry, a mother scorpion will eat her own children. After

们互相打斗，获胜者就会吃掉失败者。有时它们使用它们有毒的尾巴来杀死甲虫、黄蜂、蜘蛛和蟋蟀。

蝎子不会走很远来觅食。它们经常离家只有几英尺远，它们选定一个喜欢的地方然后晚间在这里等候捕杀猎物。如果在日出前什么也没有出现，它们将回家。蝎子的视力很差，但是它们却是很好的猎手。它们使用身体上的毛发来感受空气的运动。它们正是通过这种方式知道了猎物的存在。如果的确有什么东西靠近了，它们会用钳子抓住。

所有的蝎子都很刻薄。它们不喜欢任何人——甚至相互之间也不友好。如果饥饿的话，母蝎子能够吃掉它的孩子们。当交配后，有时母蝎子

venomous *adj.* 有毒的
pincer *n.* 钳子

wasp *n.* 黄蜂
mean *adj.* 卑鄙的

MCGRAW-HILL

mating, the female will sometimes eat the male. Small scorpions learn to stay out of the way of larger ones.

Scorpions have been crawling the earth for 450 million years. That means they were here long before dinosaurs. It's easy to see how scorpions have survived so long. They really are amazing creatures. For one thing, scorpions are almost impossible to kill. You can't *drown* them. They can live underwater for two days. And they can survive both extreme cold and heat. In one test, a scorpion was left frozen in a block of ice for three weeks. When the ice was melted with a *blowtorch*, the scorpion simply picked itself up and crawled away. Scorpions have been found on mountains as high as 16,000 feet. They have also been found in cracks in the *earth* as deep as 2,500 feet. Scorpions are independent too. They can store enough

---

会吃掉公蝎子。小蝎子要学会不要挡了大蝎子的道。

蝎子在地球上存在已经四亿五千万年了，也就是说它们比恐龙还要早得多。很容易看出它们是如何存活了这么长的时间的。它们是很令人惊奇的生物。其中一点是蝎子几乎是无法杀死的，你无法淹死它们，它们可以在水下生活两天。它们在极端的严寒和酷暑下都能够存活。在一次试验中，一只蝎子被冻在冰块中达到3个星期。当这个冰块用喷灯融化后，蝎子又苏醒而且爬走了。在16,000英尺的高山上可以找到蝎子。在地下2500英尺深处的裂缝中也能找到蝎子。蝎子也很独立。它们可以存储足

---

mate *v.* 交配

blowtorch *n.* 喷灯

drown *v.* 淹死

earth *n.* 泥土

energy to go without eating for more than a year. And they can survive almost forever without drinking water.

Scorpions, which are about two to five inches long, don't go looking for trouble with people. But these *grumpy* little bugs wear a don't-mess-with-me label. At the slightest sign of danger, they will raise their tails with their sharp stingers. They won't hesitate to strike any human being who disturbs them.

People can easily *stumble* into the path of a scorpion. Many scorpions hide out near human activity. They *lurk* in spots such as carports and woodpiles. They will crawl into sleeping bags or shoes left outdoors. That is why, if you ever camp where scorpions *dwell*, you should always shake out your shoes before putting them on. Otherwise, you might find a nasty surprise waiting for you. People

---

够一年不吃不喝的能量，而且它们几乎可以不用喝水。

蝎子大约2至5英寸长，它们不找人类的麻烦。这些脾气暴躁的小虫子戴着"别惹我"的标签。即使遇到一点点的危险，它们就会仰起带有尖利蜇针的尾巴，它们会毫不犹豫地攻击打扰它们的人。

人们很容易就能够踏入蝎子的领地。许多蝎子在人类活动的地点附近活动。它们经常在车库或者木头堆这样的地方游荡。它们可能会爬进遗忘在室外的睡袋和鞋子里面。这就是为什么当你在蝎子居住的地方野营时，在穿上鞋子前需要倒一倒。否则你会发现一个肮脏的东西等待着你。人们

---

grumpy *adj.* 脾气暴躁的
lurk *v.* 埋伏；潜藏

stumble *v.* 失足；犯错
dwell *v.* 居住

do get stung by scorpions all the time. For most healthy adults, the sting of a bark scorpion is just a painful *nuisance*. That same sting, however, can be deadly to an old person or a small child.

No one knows what little Ross Brown did. But he must have disturbed a scorpion in some way. In any case, a bark scorpion had stung him. On that long drive back from Mexico, his life was *draining away*. Don Brown, driving as fast as he *dared*, at last reached the Arizona border. Karen yelled out to the customs officials for help. Within 40 minutes, Ross was being rushed by ambulance to a nearby *clinic*. From there he was flown by helicopter to a hospital.

By the time Ross arrived at the hospital, it had been five hours since the scorpion had stung him. The doctors took one look at Ross, who was shaking and foaming at the mouth, and knew

---

确实总是受到蝎子的袭击。对于最强壮的成年人来说，树皮蝎子的叮蜇就是一次疼痛的麻烦事。但是同样的一次叮蜇对于老年人或者小孩来说就可能致命。

没有人知道小罗斯·布朗做了什么。但是他一定是以某种方式打扰了蝎子。无论怎么样，一只树皮蝎子叮了他一下。在那个从墨西哥驾车返回的路程中，他的生命正在渐渐枯竭。唐·布朗已经把车开到了他敢开的最快速度，最后到达了亚里桑那的边境，凯伦呼喊着海关工作人员寻求帮助。在40分钟内，罗斯被救护车送到了附近的小医院。在那里他被直升飞机送到了大医院。

当罗斯到达大医院时，从蝎子蜇算起已经过了5个小时。医生们看了看罗斯，他当时正在发抖，而且嘴中满是白沫。医生们马上知道发生了什

---

nuisance *n.* 麻烦事

dare *v.* 敢；不惧

drain away 渐渐枯竭

clinic *n.* 诊所

immediately what had happened. The little boy had all the classic signs of a bark scorpion sting. A doctor gave Ross a shot to *neutralize* the scorpion's poison. It worked. In just 20 minutes, the boy's *jerking* stopped and color returned to his face. *Worn out*, Ross fell asleep. Three hours later, the doctor sent him home with the happy news that he was going to be fine.

Still, it had been a close call. As the case of Ross Brown shows, the *threat* of scorpions should not be taken lightly. Some scorpions can kill.

么事情。这个小男孩身上表现出了树皮蝎子蜇过的典型症状。一名医生给罗斯打了一针来调和蝎子毒素。这一针很好使，20分钟后，孩子的抖动结束了，脸上恢复了血色，罗斯筋疲力尽地倒下就睡着了。3个小时后，医生把他送回了家，并带回了一个好消息，他很快就会好起来的。

　　但是，这是一次紧急时刻。正如罗斯·布朗事件展示出的，蝎子的威胁不应当被小瞧，一些蝎子是致命的。

---

neutralize　*v.* 使……中和
wear out　筋疲力尽

jerk　*v.* 痉挛
threat　*n.* 威胁

16

The Mystery of the Giant Squid

You don't have to see a giant *squid* to be afraid of it. All you have to do is read some of the things that have been written about it. Writers have called it a "*ghastly* looking *creature*." They have labeled it a "sea monster," a "devilfish," a "*horrible* beast."

In his story "*The Sea Raiders*," H. G. Wells said the squid's "shape

Little is known about the giant squid. Only a few dead giant squid, found by accident, have been examined by scientists. Some sailors say they have been attacked by these "sea monsters," which may grow to be 55–75 feet long.

神秘的大乌贼

关于大乌贼我们知道得甚少。只是偶然之间发现一些死掉的大乌贼才给科学家们提供了研究的素材。一些水手们说他们曾经受到过这种"海洋怪物"的袭击，它们的身体能够长到55至75英尺长。

你无须看到大乌贼来感受它的可怕。你需要做的就是读一些写到它的文章就可以了。作家们称它们是"看起来可怕的生物"。他们给它打上"海洋怪兽"、"魔鬼鱼"、"可怕的动物"等称呼。

在关于它的故事《海洋袭击者》中，H. G. 维尔斯说这只乌贼的"样

---

squid *n.* 乌贼
creature *n.* 生物

ghastly *adv.* 可怕地
horrible *adj.* 可怕的

somewhat *resemble* [es] an octopus," with "very long and *flexible tentacles*." Jules Verne described it further in his book *Twenty Thousand Leagues Under the Sea*. Verne said its "dreadful arms" are "twice as long as its body." They *wriggle* like a "nest of serpents." Verne also noted the giant squid's "enormous staring green eyes." Its mouth, he said, is like a huge pair of scissors. And its tongue is lined "with several rows of pointed teeth."

In *Denizens of the Deep*, Frank Pullen said the giant creature "does not pursue his prey." Instead, "he waits like some... spider in the center of his web of far reaching tentacles." In the novel *Beast*, Peter Benchley described a giant squid "hove [ing] in the ink dark water, waiting." In Benchley's words, "It exist[s] to survive. And to kill."

If these descriptions don't frighten you, nothing will! But these

---

子有点像章鱼，它有很长而且灵活的触手"。朱丽思·沃恩在他的书《海底两万里》中，沃恩说它"可怕的触手"有"它身体的两倍长"。它们扭动时就好像是"一窝毒蛇"。沃恩还注意到了大乌贼的"巨大的瞪着的绿色眼睛"。据他说，它的嘴就好像是一把巨大的剪刀。而它的舌头"上面有几排尖利的牙齿"。

在《海底居民》一书中，佛朗克·布伦说这种大生物"自己不追捕猎物"。"而是像……蜘蛛一样等待猎物，它的长长的触手就是蜘蛛张开的网。"在小说《畜生》中，皮特·本奇丽把大乌贼描写成"在黑漆漆的水中游荡，等待着。"用本奇丽的原话来说，"它的存在就是为了生存，为了杀戮。"

如果这些描写不能使你害怕，那么什么也不能使你害怕了！但是这些

---

resemble *v.* 类似；像
tentacle *n.* 触手

flexible *adj.* 灵活的
wriggle *v.* 扭动；蠕动

accounts come from fiction writers. How much of what they have written is *accurate*? That's not an easy question to answer. The truth is that we know very little about the giant squid. It is one of the rarest creatures on earth. It lives somewhere in the depths of the ocean, but nobody knows exactly where. Nobody has ever seen one in its natural setting. We know giant squids are down there, however, because every now and then one will come to the surface. It may get caught in a fishing net, or its body may wash up on shore.

Clyde F. E. Roper has spent more than 35 years studying giant squids. In 1995 he set up an *exhibit* for the Smithsonian Institution. He says, "We probably know more about the dinosaurs than about the giant squid." What little we do know, though, is *fascinating*.

To start with, giant squids really are giant. In 1873 one got caught

---

是小说作者的描述，它们有多大的可信度呢？这可不是个可以简单回答的问题。真相是我们对于大乌贼知之甚少。它是世界上最稀少的生物之一。它生活在大洋的深处，但是没有人知道在哪里。在自然条件下也没有人看到过一只。我们知道大乌贼在那里，因为不时地会有一只来到水面上。它可能被鱼网捉住，或者尸体被冲上海岸。

　　克莱德·F·E·洛伯花费了35年的时间来研究这种大乌贼。1995年他为史密森学会举办了一个展览。他说："我们了解恐龙的知识要比大乌贼的多。"我们知之甚少，只知道它很有趣。

　　首先，大乌贼真是很大。1873年，在纽芬兰渔民的鱼网中抓到了一

---

account *n.* 叙述　　　　　　　accurate *adj.* 精确的
exhibit *n.* 展览　　　　　　　fascinating *adj.* 迷人的；吸引人的

in a fishing net in Newfoundland. It took four men to *haul* it up out of the water. The squid's body measured eight feet long. Its squirming tentacles added another 24 feet to its length. Two years earlier, an even bigger squid had washed ashore in Newfoundland. Its total length was 52 feet. The all-time record goes to a squid in New Zealand. It measured 55 feet.

Even that may not be the outer limit. Fishermen have described giant squids as "much larger than the largest whale, even *exceeding* in size the *hull* of a large vessel." Roper thinks some may reach 75 feet. And a professor in Canada has declared that they could grow up to 150 feet!

Its length is not all that's big about a giant squid. The creature can weigh up to a ton. Its tentacles are as *thick* as small tree trunks.

只。4个人用力才把它拉出了水面。这只大乌贼的身体有8英尺长，它蠕动的触手又给它增加了24英尺的长度。两年前，一只更大的乌贼曾经被冲到了纽芬兰的海岸上。它全部的长度能够达到52英尺。最长的纪录要归于新西兰的一只大乌贼，它的长度达到55英尺。

即使这个也不一定是最大的限度。渔民们曾经描述过大乌贼"比最大的鲸鱼还要长很多，比大船的船体还要长。"洛伯认为一些能够达到75英尺长。一位加拿大的专家宣称它们能够长到150英尺！

它们的长度不是大乌贼唯一巨大的地方。它们的体重可以达到一吨。

---

haul *v.* 拖拉
hull *n.* 船体

exceed *v.* 超过
thick *adj.* 粗大的

And its eyes are the largest of any animal in the world. These eyes are bigger than dinner plates, bigger even than car *hubcaps*.

Giant squids have other interesting features. They can *squirt* black ink into the water to confuse enemies. If a tentacle is ripped off, they can grow a new one. Their bodies contain three hearts. Their brains are quite highly developed. And researchers now think they communicate with each other by quickly changing the color of their skin. At times they appear light-colored. But in a flash, they can turn red, brown, or deep purple.

There is no question that a giant squid is an *awesome* creature. But that does not necessarily mean it is dangerous to human beings. In fact, some researchers believe the giant squid is quite shy. One British scientist has called it "a *sluggish* animal". He believes it stays

---

它们的触手可以像小树一般粗细。而且它们的眼睛也是世界上生物中最大的。它们的眼睛比用餐的盘子、小汽车的轮毂罩还要大。

大乌贼还有其他的特征。它们能够在水中喷出黑色的墨汁来迷惑敌人。如果一条触手被撕扯掉了，它们还可以长出一条新的。它们的身体中有3个心脏，它们的大脑很发达。研究人员发现它们通过快速改变身体颜色来进行信息交流。有时它们近似于白色。但是在灯光下，它们会变成红色、棕色或者深紫色。

毫无疑问，大乌贼是一种可怕的生物。但是这并不意味着它对人类存在危险。实际上，一些研究人员认为这种大乌贼很害羞。一位英国的科学

---

hubcap *n.* 轮毂
awesome *adj.* 可怕的

squirt *v.* 喷出
sluggish *adj.* 行动迟缓的

near the ocean floor. It survives, he thinks, by eating the bodies of small creatures that have died and sunk to the bottom.

Other researchers doubt that the giant squid leads such a *meek* life. If it did, why would it have developed such strength? And so many powerful weapons? After all, its long arms are perfect for wrapping around a victim. These arms are filled with muscles. They could easily put the squeeze on a fairly large animal. The arms are also covered with little *suction* cups that could help the squid hold onto its prey. The giant squid's mouth is large and shaped like a bird's *beak*. Out of this mouth comes a tongue covered with so many jagged teeth that anything it touches would be ripped to *shreds*. (That is one reason why the creature's diet remains a mystery. Scientists have looked inside dead squids' stomachs but have found nothing.

家称之为"行动迟缓的动物"。他认为它就呆在海洋的底部，它能生存下来是靠吃死亡后沉到海底的小生物的尸体为生的。

其他研究人员对这个大乌贼过着这样温顺的生活表示怀疑。如果是这样，那它为什么有这样巨大的力量？而且有这样强大的武器？毕竟它长长的触手完全可以缠住受害者。这些手臂里面充满了肌肉。它们可以轻易地将一个比较大的动物缠住。手臂上还布满了可以吸吮的小口，能够使大乌贼很容易地抓紧猎物。大章鱼的嘴很大，像鸟的喙一样。在嘴里面有一个舌头，上面布满了锯齿状的牙齿，任何东西碰到了它都会被撕扯成碎块。（这就是为什么这个生物的食谱还一直是个谜的原因。科学家曾经检查过

---

meek *adj.* 温顺的
beak *n.* 鸟嘴

suction *n.* 吸；抽吸
shred *n.* 碎片

Whatever passes through a giant squid's mouth is rapidly reduced to mush.)

Over the years, there have been stories of giant squids attacking people. It is not clear if these stories are true. But they are enough to send *shivers* down your *spine*. There is, for instance, the story of *the Brunswick*. This ship was making its way across the Pacific Ocean in the early 1930s. One day, the crew spotted a huge squid in the water. It was swimming below the surface, next to the vessel. The giant squid was able to keep up with the Brunswick, which was traveling at close to 25 knots, or 30 miles per hour. Suddenly, the squid turned toward the ship. It whipped itself against the hull. Its tentacles tried to grab hold of the metal. The tentacles slipped, however, and the giant squid *skidded* forward into the *propeller*. There

---

死掉的乌贼的胃，但是什么也没有发现。无论什么通过了大乌贼的嘴都会很快就变成碎片。）

多年以来一直有大乌贼袭击人的故事。还不十分清楚这些故事是否属实。但是这已经足够使你感到恐惧的了。比如有一个《布兰思维克》的故事。20世纪30年代，这艘船当时正在横穿太平洋。一天船员们发现了在水中的一只巨大乌贼。它就在水下贴着船游着。这个大乌贼能够跟上布兰思维克号的速度，当时它的速度是25节，或者每小时30英里。突然大乌贼转向了船只，它突然向船体冲了过来，它的触手试图抓住金属把手，触手滑动了，大乌贼滑向螺旋桨。在那里，大乌贼被切成了小块。

---

shiver *n.* 颤抖

skid *v.* 打滑

spine *n.* 脊椎

propeller *n.* 螺旋桨

it was chopped into small pieces.

Another attack was reported some years earlier in Newfoundland. A group of fishermen noticed a big object in the water. They thought it might be part of a *wrecked* ship, so they rowed their small boat over to it. Instantly, the object came to life. It *rammed* the boat with its beak-like mouth. At the same time, it swung a mighty arm up, *encircling* the boat. Before the giant squid could drag the boat under, one man managed to cut off the arm. The creature then slipped back down into the water. The fishermen were left holding a writhing 19-foot tentacle.

In another report made during World War II, 12 men spent a night floating in the middle of the Atlantic Ocean. The enemy had just *sunk* their ship. For hours they clung to the edges of a tiny raft. Suddenly,

---

还有一次报告是在纽芬兰的袭击，这是早些年发生的事情。一群渔民在水中发现有一个巨大的物体。他们以为可能是一个沉船的船体，所以他们驾驶小船在上面通过。但是突然之间，那个物体活了起来。它用喙状的嘴重重地撞在小船上。同时它的一条可怕的触手举了起来，缠住了小船。巨大的乌贼正要把小船拖到水下，一个人尝试着切断了触手。这个乌贼马上滑入了水中，弃船而去，留下了一条19英尺长的还在翻腾的触手。

还有一次报告是在第二次世界大战时期，12个人在大西洋的中心飘荡着，敌军刚刚击沉他们的船只。几个小时以来，他们一直抓住一个小筏

---

wrecked *adj.* 失事的
encircle *v.* 循环；环绕

ram *v.* 猛击；猛撞
sink *v.* 下沉

in the dead of night, a giant tentacle *emerged* from the water. It grabbed one man and pulled him down, never to be seen again.

Whether or not these attacks really happened, the giant squid remains an object of fear and *awe*. As we learn more about the creature, we may find that there is no need for fear. Then we can *remove* it from the list of "Angry Animals". Or we may discover that all the *horror* stories are true. In that case, perhaps we should move the giant squid to the top of the list!

子的边缘。突然在死寂的夜晚，一只巨大的触手从水中冒了出来，把一个人拉下了水，然后就消失了。

无论这些攻击是否发生过，大乌贼一直是一个引起恐惧和惊叹的庞然大物。随着我们对它研究的深入，我们可能发现根本没有必要恐惧。然后我们可以把它从"愤怒的动物"列表中取消。或者我们也许发现所有可怕的故事都是真的。那样的话，我们可能会把大乌贼排到首位。

---

emerge *v.* 浮沉；暴露
remove *v.* 移除；移开

awe *adj.* 敬畏的
horror *n.* 恐惧

17

Bear Attack

Trouble was about to *break out* on Mount Lemmon. For years the 9,000-foot *peak* north of Tucson, Arizona, had been a popular spot for hiking and camping. In the summer of 1996, however, the mountain was not a safe place to be. Danger was lurking behind the trees and in the shadows.

In 1996 a drought dried up much of the food supply of the bears on Arizona's Mount Lemmon, causing problems with bear attacks at campsites on the mountain.

熊的袭击

1996年一场大旱把位于亚里桑那州列蒙山的熊的食物来源完全毁掉了，导致熊经常袭击山中营地。

列蒙山上出现了危机。多年以来亚利桑那州图克森市北部的一座9000英尺高的山峰一直是登山和野营爱好者们的乐园。但是，在1996年的夏季，这里却是一个不安全的地方。危险就隐藏在树丛里、阴影处。危

break out 爆发；突发   peak *n.* 山峰

The danger could be summed up in just one word: bears. A recent *drought* had dried up much of the bears' food supply. Now these animals were looking for food near human sites. Before the summer was over, two girls would learn just how *fearsome* hungry bears could be.

Jennifer Corrales was the first victim. On July 13 eight-year-old Corrales was camping out on Mount Lemmon. She had come with her Girl Scout group. They were staying at Whispering Pines campground. As night fell, the girls and their adult leaders made "s'mores." They piled chocolate bars and *marshmallows* on top of graham crackers. That made a *gooey* but delicious treat.

When Corrales finished eating, bits of marshmallow and chocolate clung to her face. She didn't bother to wash up. Instead,

---

险说到底就是一个字：熊。近来的一次旱灾使熊的食物供应大大减少，现在这些动物在人类的居住地附近寻找食物。就在夏季即将结束之际，两个女孩将亲身体会到饿熊是如何的可怕。

珍妮芙·克拉斯是第一个受害者。7月13日，8岁的克拉斯在列蒙山上野营。她是与女童子军军营一起来的。她们住在"私语林"的营地。夜幕降临，女孩们和她们的成年带头人开始玩"棉花糖"游戏。她们把巧克力块和蜜饯堆放在全麦饼干上面，这个东西很黏，但很好吃。

克拉斯吃完后，有一些蜜饯和巧克力粘在她的脸上。她没有费力气把它们洗干净，直接就爬进了她的铺盖卷，在星星下面就睡着了。

---

drought *n.* 干旱
marshmallow *n.* 果汁软糖

fearsome *adj.* 可怕的
gooey *adj.* 胶粘的

she just climbed into her bedroll. She fell asleep under the stars.

Sometime that night, Corrales woke up. A huge *hulking* shape *loomed* over her. It was a bear! The animal leaned over and sniffed Corrales's face. Terrified, Corrales screamed. The bear swiped at her face with its giant paw. Then it turned and left the campsite.

Corrales was taken to the hospital. The bear had ripped the tear *duct* in her eye. Its claws had cut her face. Still, she was lucky. The damage could have been much worse.

After the incident the Arizona Game and Fish Department made plans to trap the bear and move it to a different mountain. Officials said it had become too *bold*. The same bear had recently gone into a cabin in search of food. It had also been seen tearing into an outdoor refrigerator. Officials were sure it was the same bear. A scar

---

夜里，克拉斯惊醒了。一个巨大、笨重的身影正在她的面前若隐若现。是熊！它凑了上来，嗅着克拉斯的脸。克拉斯感到十分惊恐大声尖叫。熊用巨大的掌重击了一下她的脸。然后掉头离开了营地。

克拉斯被送到了医院。熊把她眼睛的泪管划坏了，熊的爪尖也划坏了她的脸。但是她是幸运的，本来毁坏可能会更大的。

这次事件之后，亚利桑那州的渔猎部制定了诱捕这只熊，并把它送到其他山区的计划。官员们说它太大胆了。就是这只熊，近来曾经钻入了一座小木屋中寻找食物。也有人见到它把一个室外冰箱扯坏并钻了进去。官员们确信就是这只熊，它背部的一道伤疤是它明显的标记。

---

hulking *adj.* 笨重的
duct *n.* 导管

loom *v.* 隐约可见
bold *adj.* 大胆的

on its back made it easy to spot.

But this was not the only bear on Mount Lemmon. There were others, and most of them were hungry too. Every day the bears *scoured* the woods searching for food. Some found trash left by careless campers. A few *prowled* around cabins where people lived. One woman who lived on the mountain felt sorry for the bears. She began leaving food for them on her back *doorstep*. She meant well, but she really just added to the problem. As the bears became used to taking people's food, they lost their fear of humans. That made them more dangerous than ever.

Meanwhile, 16-year-old Anna Knochel was getting ready to camp out on Mount Lemmon. Knochel was part of a 4-H group from Pima County. The group had plans to camp at Organization *Ridge*. This

---

但是列蒙山上不止有这一只熊，还有许多，而且他们中的大多数也在饥饿之中。每天熊都在树丛中搜索食物，有的找到了粗心的旅行者留下的垃圾，还有一些在人居住的房屋附近游荡。有一名在山中居住的妇女为熊感到难过，开始在后面的阶梯上为它们留一些食物，她的本意是好的，但是实际上她把事情弄糟了。随着熊习惯于吃人给的食物，它们对人的恐惧感也消失了。这使他们比以前更加危险。

当时，有一个叫作安娜·克诺奇尔的16岁女孩准备在列蒙山野营。克诺奇尔是皮玛县的一个4-H组织的成员。这个组织计划在公共活动的山

---

scour v. 走遍（某地）以搜寻某物   prowl v. 徘徊

doorstep n. 门阶   ridge n. 山脉

was a popular campground on the mountain. Knochel's group had 71 children and 11 adults. There were also 14 *counselors*, one of whom was Knochel.

On the night of July 24, Knochel was on the mountain. It was dark when she and the others went to bed. Knochel was alone in her tent, but she wasn't worried. There were plenty of people in tents right near hers.

Unlike Jennifer Corrales, Anna Knochel went to sleep with a clean face. Her tent contained no food of any kind. Yet at 5:15 the next morning, a huge black bear pushed its way into her tent. As Knochel *awoke*, the bear attacked.

The 340-pound bear *pounced* on top of Knochel. She screamed at the top of her voice, but the bear didn't *back off*. Instead, it began

---

地上组织野营，这里是这个山区很受人欢迎的营地。克诺奇尔的组织有71个儿童和11名成年人，还有14名顾问，克诺奇尔就是一名顾问。

7月24日晚，克诺奇尔就住在山上。当她同其他人去睡觉时，天色已晚。克诺奇尔自己在一个帐篷里面，但是她不担心，因为她旁边的帐篷里有许多人。

与珍妮芙·克拉斯不同的是安娜·克诺奇尔睡觉时脸是干净的。她的帐篷里面没有任何食物。但是在第二天早晨5:15，一个巨大的黑熊闯进了她的帐篷。克诺奇尔惊醒时，熊发动了攻击。

340磅重的熊压在克诺奇尔的身上。她大声尖叫，但是熊并没有退

---

counselor *n.* 顾问
pounce *v.* 猛扑

awake *v.* 醒来
back off 后退

ripping at her face and arms with its sharp claws. It sank its teeth into her shoulder and the top of her head. It also took a deep bite out of her right thigh.

"I'm being attacked by a bear!" Knochel shouted as blood poured from her wounds.

Other campers heard her cries. They ran to her tent and began *banging* on the *canvas*, hoping to drive the bear away. It didn't work. They shouted and screamed, but still the animal continued to *maul* Knochel. Someone yelled at Knochel to play dead. But that didn't seem to help, either. The bear kept on attacking her.

At last one of the adult *chaperones* came running with a handgun. The chaperone fired a bullet into the ground, sure that such a loud noise would scare the creature off, but the bear hardly seemed to

---

缩，而是用尖利的掌爪向她的脸和胳膊死抓。它咬到了她的肩膀和头的上部，还在她右大腿上咬了很深的一口。

"有熊袭击我！"克诺奇尔大喊着，血从伤口中涌了出来。

其他的野营者听到了她的呼救声。他们赶到了她的帐篷，开始敲打帐篷的帆布，希望能把熊赶走，但是不起作用。于是他们大声喊叫、尖叫，但是熊还是在伤害着克诺奇尔。有人尖声告诉克诺奇尔装死。但是也不起作用，熊还是在袭击她。

最后，一个成年的女伴跑着取来了一把手枪。她向地面开了一枪，本来这样的轰响会把动物吓跑，但是熊好像没有听到枪声一样。

---

bang *v.* 重击
maul *v.* 袭击；撕咬

canvas *n.* 帆布
chaperone *n.* 女伴

hear the *blast*.

Desperate, the chaperone took aim at the bear. This shot hit the animal and wounded it. Now, at last, the bear stopped its attack. It turned and fled into the woods.

The horrified campers rushed to get help for Knochel. A helicopter came and *airlifted* her to Tucson Medical Center. She was in bad shape. She needed surgery right away. Most of her right thigh and *buttock* were gone. She was covered with cuts and *puncture* wounds. She had also lost a lot of blood. "It was a devastating injury for her," one of the doctors later said. "This kind of severe bear attack was a life-threatening injury."

As doctors worked to save Knochel, sheriffs back on Mount Lemmon tracked down the bear. They followed the trail of blood it

---

女伴毫无办法，只好瞄准了熊。这次击中了它，它受了伤。现在，熊终于停止了袭击，它掉头逃进了树林。

受到惊吓的野营者们冲上来帮助克诺奇尔。一架直升飞机把她送到了图克森医疗中心。她的伤势十分严重，马上就需要外科手术，她大腿和臀部的大部分都被咬掉了，身上布满了抓伤和刺伤，还失了许多血。"对她来说，这是毁灭性的外伤，"一名医生后来说，"这种严重的由熊袭击导致的伤害是致命的。"

在医生忙着拯救克诺奇尔之时，警察在列蒙山上追踪那只伤人的黑熊。他们跟着它留下的血迹，大概找了一个小时。两名警官发现了熊，并

---

blast *n.* 爆炸
buttock *n.* 半边；臀部

airlift *v.* 空运
puncture *n.* 穿刺；刺痕

had left. It took them about an hour. Then two deputies *spotted* the bear and shot it to death.

Anna Knochel survived the attack, but her life would never be the same. She had to have several operations. Even then, she needed a brace to walk. Knochel also had to deal with what her father called "pretty vivid memories." He said, "She didn't lose consciousness during the attack or after the attack. Obviously, she has a lot to deal with *in terms of* the whole incident."

Still, Knochel tried to look on the bright side. "Her spirit has been an *inspiration* to her nurses, to her doctors, to her family," said her father. "You can't *sugarcoat* this kind of injury. But she's been amazing as far as how she's been dealing with this."

Later, Anna Knochel was asked if she would ever return to Mount Lemmon. She might, she said. But she wouldn't stay the night.

把它射杀。

安娜·克诺奇尔从这次袭击中幸存了下来，但是她的生活却再也不同了。她要做几次手术。即使是这样，她还是需要一个支架来协助走路。克诺奇尔还要对付她父亲称为"清晰的记忆"的困境。她父亲说："在袭击进行中和完成后，她都没有失去理智。很明显她对整个事件都有印象。"

克诺奇尔还是希望看到光明的一面。"她的精神对护士、医生和她的家庭来说都是一个激励，"她的父亲说，"你无法回避这样的事情，但是她对待整个事件的态度都是令人惊奇的。"

后来，安娜·克诺奇尔被问到是否还会去列蒙山区，她回答说，会的，但是不会在那里过夜。

---

spot *v.* 认出
inspiration *n.* 鼓舞

in terms of 在……方面
sugarcoat *v.* 裹以糖衣

18

A Jockey in Danger

People called it a *freak* fire. In 1983 a light bulb exploded in the jockeys' room at Oakland Park *racetrack* in Arkansas. The flames *trapped* Randy Romero, the only one in the room at the time. Other jockeys heard his *desperate* screams and pulled him to safety. But by that time the fire

Jockey Randy Romero celebrates a win at Churchill Downs.

危险的职业——赛马师

职业赛马师兰迪·洛麦罗正在庆祝一场在彻希尔·堂斯赢得的比赛。

人们把这次火灾叫作奇怪的大火。1983年, 在阿肯色州奥克兰公园跑马场的赛马师工作室中, 电灯泡发生了爆炸。引发的大火困住了兰迪·洛麦罗, 当时他正一个人呆在屋子里。其他的赛马师听到了他绝望的呼喊声, 赶

---

freak *adj.* 奇异的
trap *v.* 使……陷入困境

racetrack *n.* 赛马场
desperate *adj.* 绝望的

had burned nearly 60% of his skin.

Somehow Romero survived. But he had to spend months at a burn center. It was pure *agony*. Most nights he couldn't sleep. Sometimes the screams of other burn victims kept him awake. Other times he kept them awake with his screams. One of the most painful treatments involved being lowered into a pool of warm water. The doctors then *peeled* off his dead, *charred* skin. After the skin was removed, new skin had to be *grafted* onto his body. "It was a nightmare," said Romero.

The doctors told Romero he was lucky to be alive. They said that he shouldn't think about riding horses again. But being a jockey was what Romero loved. So less than four months after the fire, he was back at the track. He had to wear a pressure suit to help hold his

---

来救援，把他拉到了安全地带。但是火焰已经烧坏了他身上60％的皮肤。

洛麦罗幸存了下来，但是他需要在烧伤中心呆一段时间。他十分苦恼，在大部分的夜晚无法入睡。有时其他烧伤患者的尖叫声使他无法入睡。有时他痛苦的喊叫声也使别人无法睡觉。最痛苦的治疗是浸入温水的疗法。医生会在水中把他的烧伤死皮去除。死皮去除后，再向身体上移植新皮。"这简直就是噩梦，"洛麦罗说。

医生告诉洛麦罗他能活着真是很幸运。他们说他不应该再考虑骑马了。但是洛麦罗喜欢赛马师的职业，所以被烧伤4个月后他又回到了赛场。他需要穿一套紧身服来把新移植的皮肤固定好。但是那也没有使他离开赛场。

---

agony *n.* 苦恼

char *v.* 烧焦

peel *v.* 削落

graft *v.* 移植

new skin in place. But that didn't keep him out of the *saddle*.

The fire wasn't Randy Romero's only close call. He narrowly escaped death at least 20 times. He is in a dangerous profession. Falling off a horse can kill or paralyze any rider. In addition, if they fall, jockeys face the danger of being trampled by *trailing* horses in a race. Time after time, Romero was thrown to the ground when his mount fell during a race. Yet he was always able to walk—or at least crawl—away from such accidents.

By 1990 Romero was one of the best jockeys in the country. He had recovered from his *horrible* burns. He was winning hundreds of races each year. His mounts had won purses worth over 50 million dollars. Then trouble struck again. On October 27 Romero rode the *filly* Go For Wand in a 1 million-dollar race at Belmont Park in

---

这次火灾并不是洛麦罗唯一一次遇险事件。他至少有20次幸运地逃脱了死神的光顾。他所从事的是危险的行业，从马上跌落下来可以使人伤亡。而且如果从马上跌落，比赛中会有被后面跟上来的马踩踏的危险。洛麦罗的坐骑有多次跌倒经历，而洛麦罗也被摔到了地上。但是他总是能走，或者爬，从而逃脱厄运。

在1990年，洛麦罗是国内最好的赛马师之一。他已经从可怕的烧伤中恢复过来，每年赢得几百次赛事。他的坐骑已经为他赢得了5000万美元的奖金。后来厄运又一次光临。10月27日洛麦罗骑着一匹叫作"快马加鞭"的小雌马，在纽约的贝尔蒙特公园参加一场奖金达到100万美元的

---

saddle *n.* 鞍
horrible *adj.* 可怕的

trail *v.* 追踪
filly *n.* 小雌马

New York. Romero's horse battled a horse named Bayakoa for the lead. The two were head to head with less than 1/16 of a mile to go. Suddenly, Go For Wand's right front leg *snapped*. The horse went down hard, *tossing* Romero to the dirt.

Sadly, Go For Wand had to be put to sleep. When a horse breaks a leg, there is usually no other choice. Romero was lucky, though. He wasn't *trampled* by the other horses in the race. He did feel some pain in his side, however, so he went to the hospital to be examined. After a quick check Romero was back at the track. He rode in another race later that day. For the next three days, though, his side continued to ache. So he went back to the hospital for a more complete checkup. Doctors discovered he had eight broken *ribs* and a cracked shoulder.

Romero recovered from this accident just as he had recovered

比赛。洛麦罗的马与一匹叫作"巴亚考阿"的马争夺第一名。这两匹马以低于1/16英里的距离争夺着第一名，突然快马加鞭的右前腿踩空了，赛马重重地摔倒，把洛麦罗摔在地上。

可悲的是快马加鞭要被杀掉。如果赛马的腿损坏了，经常没有其他的选择。而洛麦罗很幸运，他没有被比赛中的其他赛马所踩踏。他感到他的体侧有疼痛感，所以他被送到医院去检查。在迅速地检查后，他又回到了赛场。在那天的晚些时候，他又参加了一场比赛。但是在后来的三天中他一直感到体侧的疼痛，所以他又回到了医院做全面的检查。医生们发现他折断了8根肋骨，而且肩部也出现了骨裂。

洛麦罗从这次事故中恢复过来，就像以前的状况一样。"兰迪是个

---

snap *v.* 断裂并发出尖利声音　　　　　　　toss *v.* 扔；抛；掷
trample *v.* 践踏　　　　　　　　　　　　　rib *n.* 肋骨

from his earlier ones. "Randy's the *bionic* man," says his wife. "He has had screws in his shoulder and ankles. He still has a *steel* plate on the right side of his face. You tell me a bone, and he's broken it."

On February 15, 1991, however, Romero came close to pushing his luck too far. He was riding at Gulf stream Park in Florida. Once again his mount fell. He was sent *sprawling* on the ground. This time he was really hurt. The *medics* rushed him to the first-aid room. A fellow jockey, Chris Antley, stopped by to see how his friend was doing. He saw Romero lying on a table, still and pale. "I thought he was dead," said Antley.

Romero wasn't dead, but his left elbow was badly shattered. The doctors in Florida tried to fix it. They put his arm in a cast and gave him exercises to do. Romero stayed in the cast for nine months.

像超人一样强健的人，"他的妻子说，"他的肩膀和脚踝的骨头中都有螺丝。他右面的脸上有一块钢板。你指哪一块骨头，他都摔碎过。"

　　但是在1991年2月15日，洛麦罗过分地利用他的运气。这次他在佛罗里达的高福斯特拉木公园赛马。他的坐骑又摔倒了。他被抬出来时四肢朝天地躺在地上。这一次他真的是伤势严重，救援人员把他送到了救护站。他的一名同行赛马师克里斯·安特里到那里去看看他的朋友怎么样了。他看到洛麦罗躺在桌子上面，一动不动，脸色苍白。"我当时认为他是不行了，"安特里说。

　　洛麦罗没有死，但是他的左肘部粉碎性骨折。佛罗里达的医生尽力来修复。他们把他的胳膊固定在支架里，给他以训练。洛麦罗在支架的帮助

---

bionic *adj.* 有超人力量的
sprawl *v.* 伸开手足躺

steel *adj.* 钢制的
medic *n.* 医师

During that time he couldn't ride. His *inactivity* caused him to gain weight. Soon he weighed 140 pounds, well over his racing weight of 115 pounds. It took Romero another four months to lose weight and get back into shape.

At last he thought he was ready to return to racing. But in the 1992 Kentucky Derby, he learned that his elbow was far from healed. As he rode that day, his elbow broke again. "It just fell apart," said Romero. This time he hadn't fallen. He hadn't banged it in any way. The *joint* just broke apart while he was riding.

Romero was in a panic. Never before had something like this happened. "I've broken my ankles, my *femur*, my jaw, my cheek, my collarbone, all my ribs,[and] my hip. I always *healed* like that," he said, snapping his fingers.

After seeing a new doctor, Romero thought he knew what had

下过了9个月。这期间，他无法骑马。他不活动，这导致他变胖了，很快他的体重达到140磅，这比他平时参加比赛时的重量115磅要重许多。洛麦罗又用了4个月来减肥，恢复到原来的体形。

最后，他觉得他可以继续进行比赛了。但是1992年在肯塔基的德比赛马场，他发现他的肘部远远没有愈合好。当天在他骑马时，肘部又骨折了。"就是突然裂开了，"洛麦罗说。这次他没有跌倒。也没有任何使劲的行动。只是在他骑马的过程中关节突然骨折了。

洛麦罗感到十分恐慌，以前从来没有发生过这样的事情。"我的脚踝骨折过，大腿、下巴、面颊、锁骨、所有的肋骨、臀骨都骨折过，但是我还是恢复了，"他打着响指说。

当请一名新的医生看过后，洛麦罗明白了到底是怎么回事。肘部没有

---

inactivity *n.* 静止
femur *n.* 大腿骨

joint *n.* 关节
heal *v.* 痊愈

happened. The elbow had not been properly set, so a bone had *shifted*. Instead of *bending* at the joint, it was bending at the point of the break.

Now Romero had to *undergo* another operation. This one took five and a half hours, but it worked. Romero made another of his *remarkable* recoveries. Soon he was back in the saddle doing what he loved most.

People later asked him why he didn't just quit. They asked why he continued to risk injury and even death. He had earned enough money to retire. "This is all I want to do," he answered. "Sure, I've had a lot of bad luck, but I've had a lot of good luck too. A lot of people are worse off than I am. I can still do the one thing I love most."

安置好，所以一块骨头的位置发生了错位。它没有在关节处弯曲，而是在断裂处弯曲。

现在洛麦罗还要进行另一场手术，这次进行了五个半小时，很有效。洛麦罗再一次很好地恢复了。很快他就又坐上了马鞍，从事他所热爱的事业了。

后来，人们问他为什么没有退休，他们问他为什么冒着受伤甚至死亡的危险还在工作，他已经有了足够的钱来休养。他回答道："这是我想做的，当然我遭受了许多次厄运，但我也经历了许多好运。很多人比我糟糕得多，至少我还可以一直做我最喜欢的事情。"

---

shift *v.* 移动　　　　　　　　bend *v.* 弯曲
undergo *v.* 经历　　　　　　　remarkable *adj.* 卓越的；非凡的

19

Canada's Lake Monster

One evening in 2004, a woman looked out over Lake Okanagan. She saw birds taking off from the water's surface. Then she heard a strange *thumping* sound. Something in the water began to splash and spray. The woman saw three shiny *humps* rise and fall. Some sort of huge creature was swimming in the lake! *Frightened*, the woman ran

This is a picture of Lake Okanagan in British Columbia. It is where the lake monster Ogopogo is supposed to live.

加拿大的湖怪兽

这是不列颠哥伦比亚欧肯那根湖的一幅图片。这是湖怪兽奥古普古应该居住的地方。

2004年的一个晚上，一位妇女向欧肯那根湖望去，她看见鸟从水面上起飞。然后她听到一个奇怪的重击声。水里有东西开始飞溅喷射。这个女的看见闪亮的驼峰起起落落。水里有种巨大的动物在游! 由于害怕，

thump *v.* 重击
frightened *adj.* 害怕的

hump *n.* 驼峰

back into her house to call for help. But then she stopped short. She didn't know what number to dial. After all, who would believe her?

What this woman saw—or thought she saw—was a lake monster. The most *notorious* lake monster in the world is the Loch Ness monster in Scotland. But Lake Okanagan in British Columbia, Canada, has one too. It is called Ogopogo. Like the Loch Ness monster, it has been seen *hundreds of* times. Some folks don't believe in its *existence*. But others are sure it is out there, hiding somewhere in this 80-mile-long lake.

The first people to see Ogopogo were the *native* tribes of Canada. Hundreds of years ago they drew pictures of what looks like a lake monster. They even had a name for it. The Chinook called it the "wicked one" or the "great beast on the lake." The Salish called it

---

这个女的跑回房间求助。但是她又突然停下了。她不知道拨哪个号码。毕竟，谁能相信她呢？

这个妇女所看到的或者所认为的是一个湖怪兽。世界上最臭名昭著的湖怪兽是苏格兰的尼斯湖水怪。但是欧肯那根湖在加拿大不列颠哥伦比亚省，也有一个。人们叫它奥古普古水怪。像尼斯湖水怪一样，人们已经见过它几百次了。有些人不相信它的存在。但是别人肯定它在那，藏在这个80英里长的湖里。

第一批看到奥古普古水怪的人是加拿大本地人。几百年前，他们画了看起来像湖怪兽的图片。他们甚至给它起了名字。切努克人称他们为"魔鬼"或者"湖面上巨大的野兽"。撒利希人称它为N'ha-a-tik，或者"胡恶

---

notorious *adj.* 臭名昭著的
existence *n.* 存在

hundreds of　数以百计地
native *adj.* 本族的；本地的

N'ha-a-tik, or "lake demon." These native people feared the *fiend*. Whenever they crossed the lake, they took a small animal with them. They would *toss* it into the lake as a gift to the monster. They hoped the monster would be pleased and would leave them alone.

When Europeans settled near the lake, they also saw the monster. In 1880 one woman said, "I saw something that looked like a huge tree *trunk* or log floating on the lake." But she did not think it could be a tree or a log. She said, "It was going against the *current* and not with it."

In 1936 two boys named Geoff Tozer and Andy Aikman spent many hours on the lake. These boys had heard about Ogopogo. They didn't believe the stories. But they changed their minds when they went on a four-day camping and fishing trip.

魔"。这些土著居民害怕恶魔。他们无论什么时候路过湖都随身带一个小动物。他们把它抛入湖中作为礼物送给怪物。他们希望这个怪物会非常高兴，放过他们。

当欧洲人在湖附近居住的时候，他们也看见了这个怪物。在1880年一位妇女说："我看见有个像大树干或原木一样的东西浮在水面上。"但是她觉得这不能是树或原木。她说，"它是逆流而不是顺流的。"

在1936年，两个叫作杰夫·托泽和安迪·艾克曼的男孩在湖边度过了几个小时。这两个男孩听说过奥古普古水怪。他们不相信这个故事。他们进行了为期四天的野营和钓鱼之旅之后，他们改变了原来的想法。

---

fiend *n.* 魔鬼
trunk *n.* 树干

toss *v.* 投掷
current *n.* 涌流；（水，气，电）流

On the first day, the boys caught a fish. They were so excited they didn't notice a large group of birds nearby. Their boat drifted closer to the birds. Then, without warning, the birds *screeched* loudly and flew straight up. A huge creature leaped out of the water and grabbed one of the birds in its mouth. Just a couple of seconds later, the creature disappeared again.

"Andy and I were scared to death," Geoff later *recalled*. "We spent the night as far up from the lake as possible. " They cut their fishing trip short and went home the next day. Geoff said the monster was about 14 feet long and as big *around* as a "telephone pole."

Like these boys, most people have gotten only a *brief* look at Ogopogo. It doesn't show up on any schedule. So people are often

---

在第一天，这两个男孩捉到一条鱼。他们非常兴奋没有注意到附近的一大群鸟。他们的船漂向了这群鸟。在没有预警的情况下，鸟群发出刺耳的声音，直接飞起来了。一只巨大的动物从水中跳了出来，抓住一只鸟放到了嘴里。几秒钟之后，这个动物又消失了。

"我和安迪要吓死了，"杰夫后来回忆说。"我们在离湖尽可能远的地方度过了一个晚上。"他们缩短了他们的钓鱼之旅，第二天回家了。杰夫说这个怪兽大约14英尺长，和电线杆差不多大。

像这两个男孩一样，大多数人都没有仔细看过这个水怪。它不是在任何时候都能出现。所以人们常常是措手不及。当人们意识到他们看到了的

---

screech *v.* 发出尖锐的声音　　　　　　recall *v.* 回忆
around *adv.* 大约　　　　　　　　　　brief *adj.* 短暂的；草率的

caught by surprise. By the time they realize what they're seeing, it's gone.

People have described the monster in many ways. Some have said it has a head like a horse or goat. Geoff Tozer said its head was "like a cow's." People have said the monster is green or gray or black or just a strange color. Its length has also been hard to *determine*. No one has ever seen its whole body at once. Some people have said it could be 50 feet long. Others say it is *closer* to 15 or 20 feet long.

But does Ogopogo really exist? Or is it just a product of people's *imagination*? In 1990, a Japanese camera crew came to find out. They brought all sorts of *fancy* equipment with them. Arlene Gaal, a writer

时候，它已经不见了。

人们用多种方式来描述这个怪物。有人说它的头像马或羊。杰夫·托泽说它的头像牛的头。人们说这个怪物是绿色或灰色或黑色或是一种奇怪的颜色。它的长度很难描述。从来没有人见过它的全身。一些人说它可能有50英尺长。另一些人说它接近15或20英尺长。

但是奥古普古水怪真的存在吗？或者说它是人们想象的东西吗？在1990年，一个日本摄像船员来弄清楚这件事。他们随身带来了各种精选的设备。阿琳·盖尔，一位写有关奥古普古水怪的3本书的作家是他们的

determine *v.* 确定
imagination *n.* 想象

close *adj.* （在时间上或空间上）接近
fancy *adj.* 精选的

of three books on Ogopogo, was their guide. One day, she said, she and the crew saw something "like a huge *serpent* moving slowly, turning in large circles."

Don Defty drove one of the cars for the crew. He, too, saw something. Defty was on high ground looking down at the lake. "You could see 30 to 40 feet away, under the water," he said. According to him, the monster "was large and looked like it had something like *flippers*." The crew hoped to capture Ogopogo's image with its cameras. But when the film came back, it only showed water being *churned* about. There was no clear picture of a lake monster. The crew kept looking, but they never got any good *footage* of Ogopogo.

向导。有一天，她说她和这个船员看见一个像大毒蛇的东西在慢慢地移动，在转大圈。

唐·戴夫开着一辆汽车来到船员这里。他也看到了什么东西。Defty在高处向下看这个湖。"你能看到水下30到40英尺远，"他说。按照他的说法，这个怪物"长得很大，看起来像鳍一样的东西。"船员希望用相机捕捉到奥古普古水怪的影子。当胶卷拿回来的时候，它只能表明水在搅动，没有湖怪物清晰的图片。船员一直在观察，但是他们从来也没有得到奥古普古水怪的录像。

---

serpent *n.* 蛇（尤指大蛇）
churn *v.* 搅动；搅拌

flipper *n.* 鳍；鳍状物
footage *n.* 连续镜头

That did not *discourage* Arlene Gaal. "I know something exists," she said. "There have been hundreds of sightings—too many to be explained away by any other cause."

In 2001 the town of Kelowna offered a *reward* of two million dollars to anyone who could take a good photo of the monster. So far no one has claimed the money. No one has taken that one nice, clear picture. Maybe no one ever will. But does that mean that Ogopogo doesn't exist? Or does it just mean that this lake monster is smarter—and perhaps a bit more shy—than people realize?

那没有使阿琳·盖尔失去信心。"我知道有东西存在，"她说。"已经有数百次的场景——太多的无法用其他理由来解释。"

在2001年基隆拿这个城市给任何能拍到这个怪物的人200万美元奖励。到目前为止还没有人拿到这笔钱，没有人拍到一张漂亮的清晰的照片，也许永远也不能有人拍到。但是这意味着奥古普古水怪不存在吗？或者说意味着这个湖怪物比较聪明——也许是更害羞——比人们所了解的。

---

discourage *v.* 使气馁；阻止   reward *n.* 报酬；酬谢